MW00629038

THE SOURCE
OF THE
PRESENT
CIVILIZATION

BY MIKOTO MASAHILO NAKAZONO

Hinomoto Masahilo no Mikoto Nakazono has spent his whole life in search of the final truth of human existence.

Since his youth he has studied and practiced many spiritual and therapeutic disciplines, always receiving the highest recognition, always searching for something deeper within them. When he was introduced to the Kototama Principle, he found the answers was searching for.

He has since devoted his life to the practice and transmission of this principle.

He writes, teaches, and has developed a therapy, Kototama Life Therapy, based on this understanding of human life.

He writes this book to bring back to present-day society the principle of life held by our ancestors.

THE SOURCE OF THE PRESENT CIVILIZATION
Mikoto Masahilo Nakazono

Note:
All quotes from the Bible are drawn from the Oxford edition of
the "New English Bible with the Apocrypha."

Terms likely to be unfamiliar are explained in the text, and the
glossary at the end of this volume will serve as a reminder. The
pronunciation of each word is also given.

TABLE OF CONTENTS

INTRODUCTION

My first book was a basic explanation of the Kototama Principle, written in the Japanese language. The original title was "Kototama: the original principle of Hinomoto Kuni". Hinomoto Kuni was the name given in ancient times to the geographical area of the modern country of Japan.

This book was published in English as "Inochi". I think readers will find "The Source of the Present Civilization" much easier to understand.

In this volume, I would like to talk about the origins of our civilization according to the records and documents of Hinomoto Kuni. These records began to be hidden systematically about ten thousand years ago for reasons we will see in the following chapters. They belong to two distinct categories: the first deals with the Kototama Principle itself, the principle of human life, and the second with ancient world history. The two categories were hidden separately.

As part of the treasure of the Koso Kotai Jingu, the oldest shrine of Japan, the world history records were entrusted to the care of the Takeuti family. The Takeuti have been the chief priests of the Koso Kotai Jingu for over ninety generations, and the hidden records of the shrine have come to be known as the Takeuti documents.

The original documents were written in the traditional Kami Yo letters on the skins of animals, on wood or bamboo supports, or even on paper made in that ancient time.

No historical record, however carefully preserved, can ever be the exact truth. There are examples of tampering with history in every nation of the world. The strong leaders of our civilization have always cut or changed the record to suit their purposes or to justify their actions. In my opinion, the Takeuti documents are a clear record or history only if you study them from the viewpoint of the Kototama Principle.

In this book, I will follow the historical chronology of the ancient Takeuti documents, reading them through my understanding of the Kototama Principle. I have studied and practiced Kototama for many years. I want to place the principle of life side by side with passages from the Old and New Testaments, and show the relationship between them. I want to show the truth of verses like: "Once upon a time, all the world spoke a single language and used the same words...". The aim of my research in this book has been to find the real meaning and to show the importance of phrases like these.

It would be impossible to decript a book as long as the Bible page by page. I will explain passages, as I understand them, to show how this and other sacred books can be studied from the viewpoint of the Kototama Principle and translated into their original meanings. The Bible, like all the books on which religions are based, is a symbolic representation of the principle of life; it explains how life manifests itself in the universe.

In the present state of our civilization, the sky, the water, the earth are polluted. This is a direct result of the content of our knowledge and the mistaken and confused idea we have of reality. If our viewpoint is confused, our society can only fall into chaos. Today, humanity expends all its energies for the satisfaction of its material desires. These desires in themselves are perfectly natural, but the way in which we gratify them is based on our knowledge and experience. Both are completely wrong.

"I am hungry; I want to eat". Very well, but what? The answer will be dictated by habit, or by the memory of a pleasurable experience. The question of health, or of what the body actually needs at that particular moment, doesn't arise. Or rather, if it arises, it will be in reference to other people's theories of what is "good for you". These theories, once again, will be based on this society's knowledge. We have no direct sense of what we should eat, decide, do at a given time. If individual pleasure is the first priority in the choices we make, it is easy to justify any crime. We have destroyed a great part of the natural resources of the earth in this search for comfort and pleasure.

The original desire is pure. Our interpretation of it, through our family habits and through our education, is utterly wrong. To satisfy our desire however we can only act upon the knowledge we have — our references, our values, our priorities. Desires of various kinds rule every aspect of our life. There are physical desires and there are spiritual desires, just as there are five physical and five spiritual senses. I will come back to this, but for now I want to make this clear: to satisfy the desires of both sides of our capacity (physical and spiritual), we rely on our knowledge. If this knowledge is confused, as it is in every aspect of society today, our actions will be wrong.

A long time ago, our ancestors perfected a principle of truth, in perfect harmony with the laws of life itself. I believe the time has come for us to return to this way. Guided by the spirit of our ancestors, I decided to write this book. I don't know how much it can help the suffering people of our society. I was content until now to study and practice the way of Kototama. I worked alone and suffered a long time before I began to understand the meaning of the Kototama Principle, and to compare its viewpoint with that of the present civilization. But I can no longer be quiet. There is too much pain everywhere, society has gone too far, and I must try to write what I know. This book is about the search for the source of life, and the way of returning to the source of our civilization.

For these reasons, and because I am ordered to do it by our ancestors' spirit, I have decided today to write this book.

The date is December 24 — Christmas eve — of the year 1983, in Santa Fe, New Mexico.

M. M. Nakazono

AN OUTLINE OF THE KOTOTAMA PRINCIPLE

The Kototama Principle was perfected 56,100 years ago. In that very ancient time, our ancestors grasped the reality of the entire universe as sound rhythm. The complete name of the principle of the fundamental life rhythms is Kototama Futomani.

When I first wrote this in 1983, I could only say that the Kototama Principle was perfected in an unknown epoch of ancient time. The ancient chronicles tell us that Sumela Mikoto ordered a gradual hiding of the Kototama Principle about ten thousand years ago, but nowhere is it said exactly when the principle was first perfected. My own teacher, the late Koji Ogasawara, taught that our present civilization would span about ten thousand years, the end of which we are nearing. If ten thousand years was necessary to perfect the scientific civilization, how much longer must it have taken to perfect the Kototama Principle?

Sensei Ogasawara could not give an actual date. Last year, I went to Carnac in France, and the stone megaliths raised by the ancient Celts told me the actual age of the perfected life principle.

The phenomena of the universe are divided by the human subjective capacities into dimensions, time and space. Once they are separated in this way, they can be perceived. Before that, there is only chaos. Once this separation is made, it is possible for us to search into the nature of phenomena, and to grasp them.

The viewpoint of modern science is *objective*. It studies the phenomena of the universe on the basis of their appearance and their visible activity. It divides them into categories and sub-categories, and examines the mechanisms and interactions of each.

But how are these objects manifested in the first place? How do we see, touch, smell what is around us?

The Kototama Principle is the principle of the life will itself, which created the very desire to research, to study and to understand phenomena. It is the principle of the human *subjective* capacities. These capacities made the original division into dimensions, time and space.

The source of the human objective capacities is the existence of the subject. The subject is the dimension of life.

The Kototama Principle is the content of the subject of the universe – and therefore the source of the human subjective capacities. The subject is the source of all existence; existence is the object. Science studies these objects, dissects them, looks at them in more and more detail through apparatus that is more and more sophisticated. But the objective, material outlook cannot reach the cause of the manifestation of those objects. Scientists do not know how objects — or they themselves — came to exist. Their viewpoint stays on the surface, it can only look at physical objects, until it reaches the end of matter — the void itself. The source of the manifestation of phenomena cannot be found in the phenomena themselves.

Instead of looking outward at the objects surrounding him, the researcher must look in. He must study his own existence, his own capacities, the very cause of his desire to search. The Kototama Principle is the content of the subject of the universe — it is the source of the subjective capacities of human beings.

As I said in the introduction, the Kototama Principle is explained in "Inochi", my previous book, and I won't go into it in great detail here. But the reader will need a few basic notions to follow the comparisons I want to make with the Bible and other ancient documents.

The five dimensions of existence

The content of the human capacities can be divided into five dimensions. The first is the source of the human physical constitution and its physical senses. To create the five senses of sight, hearing, smell, taste and touch, the a priori life rhythms pass through our a posteriori physical being, and meet the rhythms of our nervous system and brain. This is happening at every second of our lives. Our nerves and brain are tuned to a permanent synchronization: their vibration changes in response to the incoming rhythms. The rhythm that results from this meeting, expressed vocally, is the sound of **U**. Just as we humans have creative desires, the universe has a creative will. A creator needs to see his creation — and the universal life rhythms express themselves first in the creation of human life. We are the mirror in which the universe can see itself. We are created as the subject of creation.

There is a void at the center of the universe. The totality of the a priori universal life rhythms is perpetually concentrating into this void and expanding from it. This universal activity must see, must realize itself. Therefore, all the universal rhythms come into the lesser void at the center of the a posteriori human body, and give it the subjective capacity to see and to recognize the total universe. Our life has exactly the same activity as that of the universe. The rhythms of the life will and the life force are the sounds of **I** and **WI**. **I-WI** is the single source of the life of the universe. Its first manifestation is the creation of the human physical body, through the sound rhythm **U**.

This is the process by which non-manifested, a priori life rhythms become manifest in the a posteriori material world. The first expression of the totality of universal rhythms is life itself. It is a single seed, creating billions of seeds which are smaller but exactly like itself, with the same capacities. These are individual, temporary human lives. Humans die, but life itself never dies.

This individual, physical creation is the capacity of the **U** sound dimension. It is the action and the creation of human life. That is the reality of what religious people mean when they speak of God creating the world.

The source of the physical creation is the dimension of **I-WI**. Science grasps this as the activity of the "black holes" in space. The "white hole" is energy expanding from the void; the black hole is a concentration of separate existences into a central void, until they merge and become invisible to the physical, objective eye. The white hole is expansion, like light dawning in the East, the black hole is the darkening of the West.

The existence of our body follows exactly the same law as that of the universe. It is created around a central void, the gravitation of which holds the physical structure together. The human body, like every manifested existence, is maintained through the balance between this concentrating power and the expansion which allows us to express our consciousness and its capacities.

When you are standing in the center of the universe, expansion moves from right to left, and concentration from left to right. The center of the human body, like the center of the universe, is void. As they are drawn into this void, the concentrating energies collect the different elements needed for the sustenance and growth of the body. The expanding energy separates into different dimensions, creating the different elements of the body: bones, organs, muscles, nerves, skin, ...

In the a priori world, before the physical manifestation, this expanding and concentrating activity occupies the entire space of the universe. This movement is expressed in spirals, and these spirals meet to form a sort of web. Wherever expansion meets concentration, a whirlpool is formed, with a void at its center. This is a new creation. Wherever there is a void, it attracts outside energies and a new structure is created, mirroring exactly the concentrating and expanding activity of the universe.

The primary force of the universe is gravitation. When a void is created by the meeting of expanding and concentrating energies, heavier elements are drawn in by its gravitational pull. But once the void is "full", once the space that was void becomes denser than the surrounding space, the pull acts in the opposite direction and the energies expand out of the void. That is the rule of breathing, of life and death; it is the law which regulates the universe.

The spiral in the four directions, going out and coming back to the center.

If you can reach the void at the center of your self, you will see the activity of the universe and the creation of the physical world. When that gravitational force finally gives way, the energies constituting the body fall away from each other and it is death.

The void that is the matrix of physical existence is nothing — matter is nothing but rhythms around a void. That is all physical life is — but life cannot die. Death is an idea based on the **O** dimension individual viewpoint of the Kanagi principle.

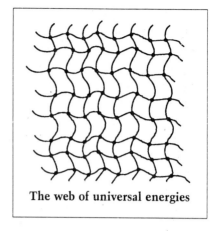

The web of universal energies

The void at the center of all creation acts through eight motive rhythms: **T K S H Y M L N**. By themselves, these rhythms have no resonance, they cannot be pronounced alone. The founders of the religions of the world knew this when they said in their different ways that you cannot pronounce the name of God.

We have said earlier that the void at the center of the white hole is the expression of **I**, and the void at the center of the black hole the expression of **WI**. This separation is made only to clarify my explanation. There is of course only one void at the center of creation. Its activity moves in two opposite directions. It is the single source of life. If these complementary actions were actually divided, life could not exist.

Around the edge (to speak figuratively) of the central void are the eight motive rhythms. The mother sound of **U**, in creating the human body and its physical senses, will synchronize with the eight father rhythms to create the eight sounds of the **U** dimension: **TU KU SU HU YU MU LU NU.**

The motive rhythms, or father rhythms, can be pronounced when they synchronize with a mother dimension:

U								**WU**
A								**WA**
O								**WO**
E								**WE**
(I	**T**	**K**	**S**	**H**	**Y**	**M**	**L**	**N**	**WI)**

Our ancestors grasped the content of the first dimension of the manifestation of our life as the a priori, unformed **U** and the a posteriori, manifested **WU**. **U** is the mother sound, **WU** the half-mother sound. The sounds created by the synchronization of father and mother rhythms (**TU, KU**, etc.) are called child sounds.

The mother sound is the total universal space of each dimension. "Dimension" means one of the facets of the expression of the life-will as expressed in the sound rhythms **U**, **A**, **O**, **E**. The father rhythms in the void grasp the mother dimension and synchronize with it, allowing it to become manifest in the child sounds. In the physical space of the human body, the rhythm of **U** becomes the sound of **WU**. It is the same rhythm, but it now belongs to the a posteriori, physical world.

In this **U** dimension, there is no real division between a priori **U** and a posteriori **WU**. **U** is the first physical manifestation, before the expansion of consciousness. The other dimensions are like a wave, rising into a greater and greater expansion, on so large a scale that our ancestors were able to grasp them in their duality, in both their a priori and a posteriori expressions.

U is the total expression of that dimension of energy in the universe. **WU** is the microcosmic expression of that energy in our individual human bodies. It is the same energy; **WU** is a fraction of the total **U**. The bridge linking the two is the eight motive rhythms.

The dimension of **I** is shown on the above sound chart, but its nature as a universal dimension is an absolute void. **I** is hidden. It is the dimension which gives their capacities to all the other dimensions, but is never manifested in itself. Black hole, white hole — both are void.

In the manifestation of human life, the first dimension to appear out of the void is **U**. With the action of the eight motive rhythms, it passes into the a posteriori world, manifesting **WU**. Eight child sounds, the a priori mother rhythm and the half-mother sound capacity: there are in all ten sound rhythms in each dimension:

U - TU KU SU HU YU MU LU NU - WU

U is the subject, **WU** becomes the first subjective capacity of the manifested human being. **WU** is the source of the capacity of the human physical senses.

The action of the eight motive rhythms gives us the capacity to divide, to separate phenomena. We can discern the expression of these eight rhythms in eight aspects of phenomena.

The dimension of **WU** is the source of the scientific viewpoint: the universe grasped and defined by the physical senses. We study the physical appearance, the external activity of phenomena. Even if we break them down into the smallest particles, no matter how advanced the technology, it always comes back to the capacity of the physical eye: what we can see.

The eight father rhythms create time and space. Each rhythm is time — what is between two rhythms is space. We can grasp space but not time. Time is a succession of single beats — the briefest blink of an eye, the cut of a razor. We can feel its dividing action, but not the actual beating. What we define as time is the lapse between two beats. This is the perception of the physical capacity.

The dimension of **U** is a chaotic dimension. All the universal energies are merged in its concentration, but the expanding action of life has not yet lit up phenomena. When we face the world from that dimension, we automatically divide it into seven. We can see seven colors; we divide our music into seven notes, eight spaces to make an octave. There are seven smells and seven tastes. Those spaces are what we can grasp with our physical senses.

In the darkness of the **U** dimension, consciousness is dim, unformulated. It is like a baby's sense of his own existence: everything blends into a general impression. We do not make a difference between self and others — that only comes with the dimension of **A**, the spiritual dimension, the expansion of light, the source of the human sense of sight.

This dimension sees further, it can grasp and judge nine divisions of phenomena. Nine divisions means eight spaces.

U can only see itself; **A** has a more complete capacity. This is why human beings, whose senses are compounded of both dimensions, can actually see eight colors. Science, with its entirely material outlook, only recognizes seven colors. The broader outlook of the **A** dimension is often interpreted as the divine spark in the human soul. From the religious viewpoint, everything that is not tangible is the gift of God.

Amatu Kanagi, the viewpoint based on the capacity of the physical senses, is called the principle of the number eight. **Amatu Sugaso**, based on the broader spiritual, mental outlook, taking in all unformed phenomena, is the principle of the number nine. But that is not yet the full capacity of human life. The source of both outlooks is the subject, **I** dimension.

The expansion of the life will, manifested in the physical dimension, is expressed by the desires of the physical senses. The concentrating activity of the life power gives these desires their strength.

The fundamental life rhythms exist in the a priori universe, and the human capacity manifests them by expressing them as sounds.

This process is the same for all the other dimensions. I will explain as we go the contents of the other subjective capacities, following the order of Amatu Sugaso.

If you tried to grasp the activity of the subjective capacities scientifically, through an electronic device, the graph or screen would only give you a picture, a symbol of this activity. It would not be the living rhythm itself. This rhythm acts and changes at every second, you cannot immobilize it and retain its essence. It is impossible to grasp the reality of life from the external, scientific viewpoint. The scientific approach is limited to the capacity of objective observation.

We can only grasp the final reality of life inside ourselves, by becoming conscious of our own inner sense and of the way in which it synchronizes with the rhythms of phenomena. Our brain's rhythm changes at every instant in response to the action of the universal life rhythms. A sight, a sound, an idea, a desire, every instant of life effects our brain's vibration. This vibration should be expressed in the sound rhythms of our speech. That is the true language, the real name of phenomena. When that rhythm is spoken, the sound comes back to the brain through the sense of hearing, and the brain, once again, synchronizes with it. There is a comparison between the original rhythm of the brain as it perceived the phenomenon, and the spoken rhythm. If the brain's rhythm is exactly the same before and after the sound, that means your recognition was perfect. It means you have spoken the truth, here and now.

That is the full human consciousness. The human being who is capable of speaking the exact life rhythms is capable of manifesting perfectly the passing moment, from a priori life energy to a posteriori existence. There is no other way to reach full consciousness.

The brain's rhythm is called **Mana**; **Kana** is the sound made by the human voice. In religious terms, Kana is the word of God.

Grasping the final truth of life means realizing that you, yourself, manifest it as it is.

Once again, I use the term "life" to mean the two directions

12

of activity of life power and life will, acting together like the front and back of the hand. Their action is separated, but their content is one. When I say "a posteriori", I mean that which can be perceived and recognized by the capacity of our physical senses. The "a priori" can be recognized and synchronized with by the capacity of our spiritual senses. Our physical senses cannot grasp the a priori world.

The capacity of the five spiritual senses

The spiritual dimension is of course also a subjective capacity. Like the **U** dimension, it can be divided into five senses:

Emotions or Sentiments (happiness, anger, sadness, ...)

Imagination needs no explanation

Intuition by this I mean a sudden idea or decision based on previous experience or knowledge.

Universal Spirit a state in which there is no individual existence. Self and surrounding phenomena become one; there is no difference between the individual and the universe.

Inspiration action of the life will. An inspiration is the direct manifestation of the pure universal subject into the here and now.

This division into five senses is my way of explaining the content of the spiritual capacity. It is my personal explanation, to try to make it easier to understand.

When I first made this division, the places of the last two senses were inverted: universal spirit came last. But later, through my practice, I found that inspiration does not appear while phenomena and self are still separate. The sense of existence of the ego has to be left behind. The dimension of universal spirit must be reached first, and then inspiration can appear.

Our a posteriori consciousness can recognize both the physical and the spiritual self. The content of this subjective capacity is the action of the life will in the dimension of **A-WA**. The life energy manifests the **A** dimension sound rhythm, and the **A** dimension is the source of our consciousness of the spiritual aspect of what we call "I am".

Like the physical dimension of **U**, this dimension appears with eight rhythms between the mother sound **A** and the half-mother sound **WA**:

A - TA KA SA HA YA MA LA NA - WA

The subjective capacity of the **A** dimension appears in this order and is expressed as the a posteriori human spiritual capacity.

The capacity of memory

Through the subjective activity of **U** and **A**, the human individual has experienced the activity of life in its physical and spiritual expressions. These experiences are stored in our memory, and this store is what we call our knowledge. Today, almost the entire content of our knowledge is the memory of our experiences in these two dimensions. What we know is what we have been told, and what we have felt for ourselves, through our physical and spiritual senses. All this is stored in our memory, and it surfaces in our consciousness when we have need of it.

The capacity of this dimension is the manifestation of our life will as the sound rhythm of **O-WO**. Once again, the eight motive rhythms make a bridge between **O** and **WO** and are expressed as **TO KO SO HO YO MO LO NO**. **O** is the subjective capacity; **WO** is the content of an individual memory. **O** is the source, the universal capacity; **WO** differs with each person's experience. Each individual human being shapes his actions according to his personal knowledge in this dimension.

The capacity of judgment

This is the capacity of the dimension of the **E** sound rhythm. Each of these dimensions is an aspect of the life will's activity: the life will **I** and life power **WI** appear through the separate dimensions of **U A O E**. These dimensions are different manifestations, but the source is always the same. **I–WI** is the subject. **E**, like **U**, **A**, and **O**, is a subjective capacity.

As in the other dimensions, the contents of this dimension's activity can be grasped in the eight child sounds between **E**, the mother sound, and **WE**, the half-mother sound:

E - **TE KE SE HE YE ME LE NE** - **WE**

I explained earlier that we base our actions on our stock of **O** dimension knowledge. We memorize, then we make a judgment on the basis of our experience. Therefore, the level of our knowledge determines the level of our judgment.

Human morality is based on the judging capacity of the **E** dimension. Morality, ethics, discernment are **WE** capacities based on our experience in **WO**, which in turn is based on the perception of the physical or spiritual senses. A person who lives for the gratification of his physical desires will have a very different judgment from another, who lives for the spiritual desires. The second will have a higher morality, but will still not reach the highest judgment.

Life will and life power

This is the real source of human life. This is the pure source of the total capacity of our being, in its physical and spiritual expressions. It is the source of the appearance of all human capacities.

The content of the life will is the sound rhythm of **I**. This is the rhythm of the expansion of our life energy from the central void. At the same time, outside elements or energies are being drawn into the void. If these expanding and concentrating activities could exist independently, both would be in darkness. But they are the two complementary phases of a single activity, and it is their meeting which sparks the energy of light. This is the light of life, the awakening of consciousness. By this light, we recognize the phenomenal universe.

Second by second, all the energy of the universe is drawn into the center of our physical body — the gravitational void at the core of our existence, tiny mirror of the central void of the universe. We grasp this concentrating activity as the sound rhythm of **WI**. That is the essential, pure rhythm of life power.

I, the expanding life will, has the capacity of grasping, of recognizing **WI**.

15

WI is the enduring life power which holds together our physical body; **I** is the expansion of the life will, the expansion of light, the expansion of desire. This activity as a whole is the source of our life.

WU WA WO WE, the half-mother sounds, have no consciousness. Only the subject, **I-WI**, and its subjective capacities **U A O E**, can see and recognize. They are the beginning of consciousness.

The order in which these dimensions are manifested in the a posteriori finite or material world determines the type of consciousness expressed by an individual or a society. We have already seen that the judgment based on the memory of physical experience is not the same as that which is based on the spiritual. There are three orders of the mother sounds, creating three different viewpoints and therefore three different types of society. We will look at them more fully in a later chapter. All three of these orders begin with the sound of **A**. **A** is the torch that lights the world — we see the world through its activity. Phenomena have no consciousness; the mountain cannot recognize itself or you.

The half-mother sounds have their expression in our physical and spiritual senses. They are the different aspects of our physical body, but they have no consciousness of their own source. That consciousness only resides in the mother sounds.

WI holds life together, but it is **I** that grasps life through the highest judgment in the dimension of **IE**.

The subjective **A** is reflected into the objective **WA**, like two mirrors facing each other. **WA** manifests the physical senses, and can look outward toward the phenomena, even if it cannot realize its own source. But **WI** is blind because its nature is the absolute void.

At the point of greatest concentration, the energy of the universe explodes again into expansion. That moment is the life rhythm of **I**, it is the subject of our existence and the subject of the existence of the universe. Our life will as human beings is the same as that of the entire universe. If we search and practice according to the Kototama Principle, this slowly becomes clear. Every human being has the capacity to recognize the source of life. The life will of **I** will grasp the existence of **WI** in the activity of **WU WA WO WE**, the half-mother sounds.

Standing in the place of the subject, it is possible to see the energies of **WU WA WO WE** as they come into the void, and so to infer the existence of their expanding action in **U A O E**. It is impossible to realize one's self without seeing clearly the activities of the **WU WA WO WE** dimensions. All the energies of the space of the universe come into our physical space, and we can witness their synchronization.

I see the activity of **WA**, therefore I am **A**. **WO** is one of my capacities because I am the expanding **O**. It is possible, in this way, to recognize the activity of the entire universe.

Once again, to clarify my explanation, I am separating the dimension of life into the expansion of **I** and the concentration of **WI**. But this dimension is one, it is the single source of life in all its physical and spiritual manifestations. **I** and **WI** are two complementary directions of one activity: its opening and its closing. The life power of **WI** is the concentrating side of the four dimensions of universal energy. **I**, the life will, is their expansion. The void of **WI** is the source of all the capacity of life.

Around the void are eight motive rhythms, four of which have a concentrating nature and four an expanding nature. The creation of the human body is the result of the action of the total universal energy. All the life rhythms of the universe are expressed in our physical constitution. In the center of our body is a lesser void, of exactly the same nature as the central void of the universe, and acting with the same motive rhythms. This is the manifestation, second by second, of the life will of the entire universe as it appears in an individual human being. This is the pure, the essential subject of the human and of the universal life.

Our source, our roots are the same as those of the universe. Our center and that of the universe have the same nature, and their activity is the same. The activity of the eight motive rhythms divides all the phenomenal world — including the space of our own body — into dimensions, time and space. The same capacity makes it possible to recognize these divisions with the a posteriori subjective capacity of our spiritual and physical senses.

The Subjective Capacities

I explained earlier that the activity of the four dimensions of the **U A O E** sound rhythms is the subjective capacity of our being, and that they act through the eight motive rhythms. I would like to explain this a little more clearly.

We have already seen the way in which life power expands as

life will. The moment of this expansion is the sound rhythm of **A**. **A** is the expanding aspect of **I**, it is the dimension which lights up the universe. It is what Jesus called the light of life.

In the a posteriori world, this energy is the awakening of the consciousness of the cerebrum, or large brain. Electrical current is one form of energy, but it cannot manifest itself without wires or bulbs.

A is only the light. Without the eight motive rhythms of **I**, the light of **A** has no consciousness, and cannot be a subjective capacity. From the a priori world of unformed phenomena, it is the activity of the eight motive rhythms which manifests the human spiritual capacity.

The dimension of the **O** sound rhythm is the continuation of the activity of the life will **I**. Without this continuity, the light of **A** would only be a single spark — and then nothingness. Our consciousness would awaken for one instant, then sink back into darkness. There would be no possibility of life, and no expression of our capacities.

In fact, once the brain awakens, its activity never stops until death. The awakening itself belongs to the **A** dimension; the continuity of its activity, through the eight motive rhythms of **I**, belongs to the **O** dimension. **O** is the continuity of **I**. In this dimension, every experience born of the synchronization between subjective capacity and object, every physical and spiritual experience, is stored in our memory. Not only the brain, but every one of our cells has its memory. The eight motive rhythms of **I**, the life will, create this as one of our subjective capacities.

The **U** sound rhythm is the continuing expression of the life power of **WI**. All the energy of the universe merges into the void of **WI**, then springs back into the expansion of **I**. The very first moment of **I**'s life activity is the sound rhythm of **U**. The concentration is still coming in; **I** is just beginning to express itself. **U** is the first stirring of life, then comes the expansion of **A**. **UUUA** creates **WA**, the objective mirror of our existence.

A is the light of expansion. Just before this expansion, **U** begins its unconscious life. Since its expression comes before the light of the **A** dimension, **U** cannot realize its own existence. The dimension of **U** is chaos, there is no separation between subject and object. In this state of being, it is possible to sense the existence of ... something, but it is impossible to see or judge it.

"In the beginning, when God made heaven and earth, the

earth was without form and void, with darkness over the face of the abyss ..." (Genesis 1:1-2).

The sound rhythm of **U** is the origin, the real source of the five physical senses. In our practice of Amatu Iwasaka, we always begin with this sound in order to return to the source of the physical senses. Then, out of the synchronization of **I** and **WI** comes the light of **A** dimension, its continuity in **O**, its discernment in **E**. These are the human subjective capacities, from which it is possible to recognize our self.

In the dimension of the **U** life rhythm, our senses are still asleep. This dimension is like the life of an egg: it is alive, all the potential is there, but there is no activity. It cannot know itself; there is life but no consciousness.

I have explained that **I** dimension acts through eight motive rhythms. The dimension of **E** is the activity itself of these rhythms. When **I** expands, the activity of the eight father rhythms is the dimension of **E**. **E** is the creator; its activity creates the time, space and dimension of phenomena. It determines the dimension of mother rhythm to which they belong, the space they occupy (determined by the area influenced by the activity of the central void), and the time the phenomenon will last (also determined by the force of concentration of the central void). Creation means division — it is the separation of a phenomenon from the chaotic mass of universal energies, and its positioning in dimension, time and space.

The activity of **I–E** is the highest dimension of the human capacity. From this viewpoint, it is possible to recognize the source of our existence in the **U** dimension of life power, and grasp it as the sound of **WI**. That moment of recognition is the action of the eight motive or father rhythms: **IE**. The order of the activity of **IE** is **TI KI MI HI LI NI YI SI**.

It must be understood that **I-WI** is one activity. The life power of **WI** is behind the life will of **I**. **I–E** is also the action of the eight motive rhythms and the origin and the subject of human life.

This activity of the life will synchronizes with the four dimensions of energy as they come into our body, concentrating toward the void at the center of our physical being. Our activity faces that of the universe. Our concentration grasps expanding energies, they leave the central void of the universe to come toward us. This exchange goes on at every moment between all the dimensions. We breathe in oxygen and breathe out carbon dioxide, plants breathe in carbon dioxide and breathe out oxygen.

The universal expansion is the rhythm of creation, as these dimensions become the mother rhythms of **A O U E.** When they are "caught" in our gravitational pull, or grasped, each dimension's energy appears in our physical being as the half-mother sounds of **WA WO WU WE**. These are the a posteriori subjective capacities, and the sound of **WI** becomes the source of our physical constitution.

There is a progression from the a priori to the a posteriori world. From the point of view of the first subject, the **I** dimension, **WA WO WU WE** are the objects, and **WI** is the universal life power. From the a posteriori viewpoint, **WA WO WU WE** are what we mean when we say "I, myself". They are our subjective capacities, and **WI** the source of our physical existence.

Ten thousand years ago, our ancestors began to hide the Kototama Principle. Five thousand years ago, this was nearly completed and all over the world, the subjective capacities had come to be taken for the subject. Our notion of our self has become our perception of the capacities of **WA WO WU WE**. We can reach no closer to the source. Today, we say "I am", without knowing that a real universal source, a real "I" exists. We can only recognize what we have experienced through our limited level of individual consciousness.

Summary of the capacities of the five dimensions

The fundamental activity of the five dimensions of life energy is the creation of the human body and the expression of the human capacities.

From the time the Kototama Principle was hidden from human society and only referred to symbolically, the content of this activity of the five dimensions was explained through the names and stories of the gods, and through the old sciences like numerology. The basic principle of life was translated into symbols and handed down from generation to generation until today. As a result, present day men and women no longer know what a human being is. We have no answer to this most basic of questions.

Our inner capacity, like the activity of the five dimensions of life in both the finite (material) and infinite (spiritual or mental) worlds, is divided into dimensions, time and space. We, as humans, have the capacity to make this activity separate and to grasp it as the existence of the phenomenal world. Today, humanity has become incapable of grasping the reality of this recognition. Humans have no sense of their real capacity, no confidence and no knowledge of the essence of their being.

The phenomenal world only exists through the human capacity of recognition. Humanity must stand firmly on this viewpoint, and know that this is true with all its confidence. Only then can we understand the reality of life.

The people of this civilization take their capacity of recognition for the existence of an independent phenomenon. They see the objects around them without knowing of the link between their own existence and the existence of the phenomena. Humans give what they see symbolic names taken from an intellectual language and look no further into the nature of the world around them. These names have no relation to the sound rhythms of phenomena. The real name is the one which expresses the life rhythm of the named object.

The content of our modern knowledge is completely confused. No aspect of society is left intact. Our civilization is rushing along a road that leads to greater and greater sacrifices, and will not stop until all life on the surface of the earth is extinct. It is not enough to try to correct some of the mistakes. The whole outlook of society must be changed.

From the beginning of our era, our ancestors prophesied that this direction, the material and scientific civilization, must lead to great sacrifice. They announced this and today every human being sees life destroyed around him every day. Everyone feels this is wrong and would like to stop it before it goes too far. But they know no other way of life. They cannot stop this current because they can offer nothing better.

The only way to reverse the present current is to purify the content of human knowledge. To achieve this, one hundred and forty-four thousand people at least, the world over, must study the Kototama Principle. They must grasp it completely and wake up the eye of their inner source. From this viewpoint, they can reach an absolute confidence in the capacity of humanity as the subject, the creator of the universe.

We created the way of sacrifice, we can also create the perfect civilization.

144,000 leaders must appear in our society and begin to guide the world. If they do not, if our human knowledge and viewpoint cannot be purified through the Kototama Principle, our society will go on in its present course until its end. There are many ways for us to commit suicide with science. The air, the water can be destroyed completely, sacrificed to our material desires. It will mean the end to all life on earth. From the beginning of recorded history, all the world's religions have announced that day – and we who are alive today risk seeing it.

The principle of Kototama is the principle of the human life dimension, and the highest human truth. This principle belongs to all human beings; every human has the same capacity.

There are of course different levels of truth. We say "I love you" and mean "I want your body" or "I am impressed by your social standing" or "I want something from you". That is a careless, cheating way of speaking. It is not the real human language. How is it possible to communicate, how can we build a perfect society on the basis of our uncertain, equivocal languages?

You can say that if language itself is a lie, it is impossible to tell the truth. But the truth exists, and resides in the permanent expression at the core of every human being, in their **I** life will dimension. This dimension is our origin, our seed. It comes before the separate expressions of the spiritual and physical dimensions of **A** and **U**.

It is very difficult to open the eye of our seed. It is impossible without serious discipline and practice. The student must follow the correct order of practice if he is to make any progress at all.

Our ancestors perfected their practice fifty-six thousand years ago, but it was hidden with the principle itself. The leaders of the world met and agreed to hide temporarily the complete order of the principle, and to guide the world's activity into the material, scientific civilization. This process was begun ten thousand years ago. It started slowly and gathered momentum, until the real crusade for the new civilization was undertaken between three and four thousand years ago, in the time of Moses.

From that time on, the entire world was educated through symbols. Human knowledge became something to be acquired intellectually, or through one's own experiences. This turned humanity away from the reality of life, until the symbolic explanation came to seem the only possible truth.

But the reality of life continues to manifest itself at every moment at the core of human life. We are alive; and life itself is the ultimate truth. That is something humanity must realize if it is to save itself.

Today, everyone can feel our society is on a dangerous road. We know something must be done, but we don't know what to do. We try to find an absolute truth, but something is always missing — we don't know which way to turn. The difficulty is that we can no longer base our search on the references or knowledge to be found in today's society. Without the right principle and the right teachers, it is impossible to grasp the essence of the human seed. The way back to the source is exactly opposite to the road we are following today.

A teacher of the principle can direct his students toward the source. He can explain its content. But the truth itself cannot be grasped in another person's explanation. It only becomes yours when you grasp it in the activity of your own life. I can try to explain how I practice, what kind of exercises I do and what I experience as I do them, but I can never make someone else feel the actual sense of my practice. I can never make anyone else feel what I felt when I touched one particular stone among the thousands at Carnac.

A student can listen to the best teacher for his entire life, but it will not help him. It is only through long and serious practice that he can actually understand what his teacher is telling him. The truth is there inside him; it is his responsibility to reach it for himself.

The source is the same for everyone, the truth is the same for every human life. It is inside every one of us and it is identical for every human being. It is the reality of our existence. If you have a human body, if you act through physical and spiritual capacities, this truth is at the core of your being. The difficulty lies in getting to it.

To grasp it means to awaken the eye of your own essence, which is the universal human seed. When this is done, you will know exactly who and what you are. You will have no more doubts, no more questions.

To guide us toward this realization, to educate us, our ancestors perfected the Kototama Principle. Then, at the opening of the material civilization, it was slowly hidden and translated into the symbols and parables which are the origin of all the religions and mythologies of the world. The oldest religions, the oldest books are all symbolic explanations of this principle. The further back you go, the closer you come to a time when the Kototama Principle was still known. The oldest mythologies and chronicles make the best textbooks for modern students of the principle. They must practice re-translating them into their original meaning. To do this, to see clearly the content of their symbols, it is only necessary to change our angle of vision: to look at them from the correct viewpoint.

The first step on the road back to the source is to stand in **NAKA-IMA**. Translated into our modern language, this means "here and now", but that is not the full meaning of the sounds themselves. Pure sounds cannot be explained; **NA** is **NA** and **KA** is **KA**. I will try, in the inadequate words of the English language, to give an idea of the real meaning of Naka-Ima.

The life will of **I** dimension acts with eight motive rhythms, synchronizing with each dimension, locking into them like the cogwheels of a machine. This activity creates time and space: **IMA**. **MA** is space, **IMA** the space of the activity of **I**. The rhythm of **IMA** is a perpetual sparking, appearing as inspiration in Mana, Mani, Man, the original rhythm of our brain's activity. The space of that inspiration is **NAKA**, appearing in the Mani space of our large brain as our consciousness. The real meaning of Naka-Ima is therefore inspiration, directly from the activity of the universal life rhythms, appearing here and now in the space of our human mind.

As I explained before, the finite and infinite phenomenal worlds are divided into dimensions, time and space. We grasp phenomena when they appear as independent, separate existences — but it is our recognition which separates phenomena and gives them their individual existence. That is the capacity of the subject, facing the phenomena as objects. The subject is **I**, the life will, with the activity of its eight motive rhythms. Naka-Ima is this activity of **I** dimension, synchronizing with the energies of each dimension, and creating each spark of phenomenal existence. In this way, the phenomena appear and are divided into dimensions, time and space.

In other words, Naka-Ima is the moment of the creation by **I** of the different dimensions, of time, and of space. Naka-Ima is the space for the creation of the phenomenal world as a whole.

It is not enough to know that Naka-Ima means "here and now". That is only an intellectual concept, it is completely different from the real meaning of the sounds, and from the actual practice of Naka-Ima. The best way to practice standing in Naka-Ima is Zen meditation, facing the void. Christ called it "being like a little child". The words are different but the meaning is the same. It is a state in which there is no knowledge, no references, no memory. In this practice, you throw them all away, and become like a blank page. You can then begin to see the activity of life, as it is.

Our ancestors stood in this moment of Naka-Ima and recognized their own life will in **I** dimension. They saw how it expressed itself and how it synchronized with the energy of universal space. They saw this, not through their physical eyes, but with the eye of the seed, the universal source of life. Through their Mani brain rhythms, they perceived how the life will made all phenomena appear to their physical and spiritual eyes. When they saw how the motive rhythms synchronize with the energies of the different dimensions, they saw the fifty sounds, and they completed the principle of Kototama Futomani.

They arranged this principle, the total expression of human life, into three orders of mother sounds. The understanding based on the physical senses became the order of Amatu Kanagi: **A I U E O, WA WI WU WE WO**. The understanding based on the spiritual senses became the order of Amatu Sugaso: **A O U E I, WA WO WU WE WI**.

Something is still missing in both of these orders. We are more than the sum of our physical and spiritual perceptions. To reach the complete human capacity and the consciousness of the dimension of life, there is only the order of Amatu Futonolito.

In the beginning, the student can put himself in Naka-Ima intellectually, thinking: "I am at the center of the universe, here and now". He can place himself at the center of the universal sights, sounds, smells by opening his senses and receiving all the energies they can grasp. The eyes are particularly important — there is always something to see. (Much of what can be seen is artificial, and it is best to try to synchronize with natural phenomena — sky, mountains.) The student then tells himself that without his recognition, they do not exist. He is the creator, his recognition creates every thing.

Intellectually, it is impossible to believe this. From the objective viewpoint, it could as easily be the other way around. Why should it not be the sky who created you? But with practice, you will come to see why our ancestors said this. Try to stand always, here and now, at the center of the universe. The **I** dimension in you is synchronizing with all the outside energies. Slowly, you will come to recognize this. This exercise is only based on the **U** dimension, but it is the beginning of your practice.

People in a scientific culture are attracted by phenomena. They see something and immediately want to take it apart to understand how it works. "What is this? A mountain! How interesting. We will dig to see if there are valuable minerals, and label all the trees".

They call it a mountain because they were shown pictures in school, and taught that this was a mountain. The Kanagi viewpoint believes it has explained something when it has named it. But it is impossible to know the exact meaning another person puts into a word. Every word is laden with our own individual experiences, likes, dislikes. It is impossible to communicate these nuances, and this gives rise to endless conflicts. The only perfect communication is in the pure sounds of Kototama, the life rhythms themselves.

People accept the word "mountain" in one country, "yama" in another, without question, and look no further into the actual nature of the mountain. But how does a human being see a mountain? Science now says that matter can be broken down into smaller and smaller particles until one reaches the void. If the essence of matter is void, what is it I am seeing at every moment, and what makes me see it?

You are standing in the position of the seer. The mountain is a group of rhythms, expanding in space without consciousness or intention, until it is drawn into the void in your center. There, the **I** life rhythm synchronizes with it. You actually see this mountain when the rhythms have expanded out of your center, when they have "gone back" after this synchronization. The gravity power in the void center of your body catches these rhythms. This information passes through your nervous system and is transmitted to your sense of sight, which can realize it. A phenomenon belonging to another dimension would have called upon your ears, or your sense of touch.

This is still only the material vision of Kanagi. Your eyes cannot see what is on the other side of the mountain. The energy of other phenomena exists beyond the mountain, but it is shut away from your physical sense of sight. The rhythms that can be perceived by the human senses are only a limited category. There are however other ways of synchronizing with the rhythms of phenomena.

Practice the physical approach first, putting yourself in the center of the material world. Be certain that you are the seer, the one who recognizes. Then awaken the spiritual "I am" by putting yourself in the center of the spiritual world. Place yourself in Naka-Ima and receive the phenomena of both these dimensions. Behind them is the real seer, **I** dimension.

In the dimension of **A** reside the phenomena of each individual's subjective capacity. These are phenomena without form, without material existence. When we were speaking of the material world, we said that no two people saw the same mountain. The subjective capacity of the **A** dimension is not yet real existence: it is still individual. **A** is only an expression of the real seer, the life will. A priest, facing a spiritual phenomenon, will name it Jesus, a Buddhist will name it Buddha. No two priests will see the same image of Christ, no two artists will give him the same face. The visions are created by our capacity; the capacity to see these visions comes from the dimension of life.

The phenomena that appear are true — that is to say they are actual life rhythms of the **A** dimension, grasped by human beings. Each person, however, is interpreting them with the knowledge of his **WO** dimension. The phenomena of the mental, spiritual, unformed world belong to a much broader dimension than the phenomena of the material world, but the real source, the real subject is not there. **A** is only an individual subjective capacity. The life will is behind the **A** dimension phenomena, giving them their existence.

Try to find how the **A** dimension connects with the life will. Once they are connected, inspiration can come out. No one can help you do this, no one can explain it to someone who has not had this experience. You must find it for yourself. Only then can you see the sense of the words by which others have tried to explain it. Until then, they will mean nothing, they will only be lies. It is impossible to grasp the content of the Kototama Principle unless you stand in Naka-Ima. Only there can you grasp the final truth, the real source and reality of your life. Stand on this viewpoint, hold on to this consciousness, practice without letting yourself become discouraged.

I can only wish that many people will want to find this consciousness, and will have the courage to keep practicing, until the end of their lives if necessary. That is the only way for humans to reach their own life dimension.

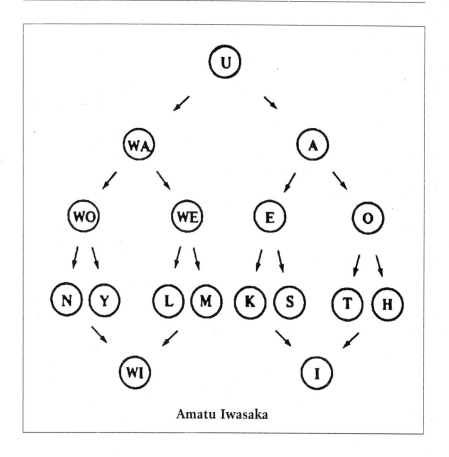

Amatu Iwasaka

Our far ancestors grasped the way in which the a priori life capacities are manifested in the a posteriori world, here and now in Naka-Ima. They grasped the content and the progression of this process and reached a total knowledge of the activity of their life. They structured this knowledge into the order of **Amatu Iwasaka**.

When it was decided to hide the Kototama Principle, to disguise it and refer to it only in symbols, the chart of Amatu Iwasaka was translated into a hierarchy of gods.

The ancient Japanese Shintoism (Ko Shinto) called this chart the seventeen hidden gods. This referred to the structure of the chart as well as the progression of sounds.

In ancient texts, this chart appears in Katakana characters as a pantheon of gods. Modern-day Japanese people are still familiar with their names: **U** is Amenominakanusi no Mikoto, **A** is Takami Musubi no Mikoto, **WA** is Kami Musubi no Kami. They have learned these names in school, but have no idea of the actual content of Amatu Iwasaka.

The I Ching hexagrams in China and the Buddhist imagery in India also follow this principle. Both are symbolic representations of the seventeen a priori sounds of Kototama.

When our ancestors, standing in Naka-Ima, succeeded in realizing their own human manifestation from the a priori to the a posteriori world, they grasped it in this order and created this chart. Students of Kototama must practice this order. It is the way which leads us back to our own origin, back to the source of life in **I** dimension.

Once you have arrived there, try to come back from the life source to the physical manifestation by following the same order in reverse. To understand your own manifestation fully, you must grasp the full cycle, coming back from **I** through the eight motive rhythms to the dimensions of **E**, **O**, **A** and **U**. Practice going from your physical existence in **U** to **I**, your source, and then back from **I** to **U**.

The name of Amatu Iwasaka, the "seventeen hidden gods", means that these sound rhythms all belong to the a priori world. **U** dimension, the first obscure awakening, the very beginning of physical manifestation, is on the border between a priori and a posteriori.

When first you begin to practice, it is very difficult to grasp the progression of these sounds and the content and activity of each dimension's subjective capacity. Many people grow tired and give up, never reaching complete certainty of the subject.

Many others miss the seer's side: **U A O E**, and see only the picture: **WU WA WO WE**. It is much easier to let your attention be drawn to the phenomena, but it means losing your concentration, and forgetting the true question: the contents of your own subjectivity.

How does a human being see phenomena? If the search is limited to examining the pictures that appear before the physical or spiritual eyes, it is impossible to find the way back to the source. Fascinated by the surface of things, you cannot go any deeper. But when the way to the source is found, then, on your return to your physical manifestation, you will find that the content of each dimension's subjective capacity is perfectly clear. You will see how your life is expressed, and in which dimension you are acting, at any moment: "This is the action of my **O**, or my **A** dimension; I can see the way in which they behave, their origin, and their content". Then you will see that the Amatu Iwasaka order of practice is perfect — that it is the only way to practice.

The activity of the eight motive rhythms of the **I** life will dimension is the source of the human self. It is the ultimate subject, the eye capable of grasping the entire phenomenal universe as it is manifested by human recognition. To see and to know this with complete certitude is to stand at the center of this manifestation as the creator of the dimensions, the creator of time, the creator of space. That is the viewpoint of the god-man, standing at the center of the universe.

As you stand in Naka-Ima, the total energy of universal space will in its concentration come into you as your own life power. It is possible to see this activity. From that standpoint, you can awaken your own self and find behind it the life will of **I**. Then, with the activity of the eight motive rhythms, start dividing these energies into dimensions, time and space. This act of separation, symbolized by the sword, is the subjective capacity of the **E** dimension.

As the rhythms of universal energy come into your center, the subjective capacity of **E** dimension separates and structures them, arranging and judging them according to dimension, time and space. Each phenomenon is set in its proper place: the sun is here, the moon is there, and here are the stars. Each phenomenon is manifested in the dimension to which its rhythms belong. The capacity of its central void will determine its time or life span, and the space it occupies.

This applies to the a priori phenomenal universe, to the spiritual human capacity, and to the a posteriori phenomenal world. The activity of **E** goes from the world of life rhythms to the material universe.

"A priori" means what cannot be grasped by the capacity of the physical senses; "a posteriori" refers to what can. Both sides are defined by the activity of the dimension of the **E** sound rhythms. When the Kototama Principle was hidden, the subjective capacity of the **E** dimension was symbolized by the double-edged blade. The sword of **E** cuts on both sides: a priori, a posteriori.

In the Amatu Iwasaka chart, the life will **I** and life power **WI** stand in a void, then come the eight motive rhythms. The total energy of the universe is drawn into **WI**. To the scientific eye, **WI** is only a void, there is nothing there, only a power of gravitation.

It is true that there is no material existence in the void, but all the life rhythms of the universe are there, merged all together in the extreme concentration of **WI**.

I and **WI** synchronize as naturally as we breathe in and out, and the eight motive rhythms are expressed. These father sounds cannot be pronounced by themselves, but they begin their action with the expansion of **I**: **TI**, **KI**, **SI**, **HI**, ...

The eight motive rhythms are the rhythms of the void. It is through their action that the life will of **I** dimension can realize the source of life power, and grasp it as the **WI** sound rhythm. The eight motive rhythms are a bridge between **I** and **WI**.

The four dimensions of energy, in spite of their different natures, all breathe in and out, expand and concentrate in the same way. They follow their law of activity and synchronize together. Every aspect of their manifestation is the creation of the life will and life power of **I-WI**.

I-WI is the human seed — the single seed from which all humanity springs. It is made up of the activity of the four dimensions of the energy of the universe. These dimensions expand and concentrate. As these two directions of activity cross each other's paths, their meeting creates whirlpools of energy, turning around a central void. That is the creation of individual lives.

All the universal elements are there in each human life, duplicating the activity of the universe itself. The nature of the central void is the same whatever its power or size. It draws in the four dimensions of energy and they expand again, driven by **I**, the life will with its eight motive rhythms. Each individual life exists separately from the central void of the universe, but its rhythms are exactly the same. Its dimensions of expression are of the same nature as those of universal energy.

Individual existences are created whenever two directions of universal energy meet and synchronize, creating a void. These lives act in the opposite direction to that of the central void of the universe. It is like a small mirror facing the sun.

The individual human can receive the universal dimensions of energy, grasp them and show their expression like a picture on the screen of the subjective capacities of **U** and **A** dimensions.

The a priori and a posteriori worlds face each other like watcher and screen. The individual life is the mirror in which universal life can see itself. We are life's eyes. We, in our physical constitution, are the objective representation of the capacities of life.

I-WI receives all of the universal energy and recognizes it through the a posteriori human capacity. It is in this way that the a priori world is manifested.

Some of our elders in the practice of Kototama have called **I-WI** dimension the "parent sound rhythms". The dimension of **WI** is the mother of our human body. It creates the energy which builds and holds it together. At the point of greatest concentration, the direction of the activity of life is reversed into an expansion which divides the phenomenal world into dimensions, creates time and space, and grasps their manifestation. That is the life will of **I** dimension, the expression of the father rhythms. The eight motive rhythms of **I** dimension are called the father rhythms; **A O U E** are the mother dimensions.

I acts through the eight father rhythms when it divides and grasps phenomena. That aspect of **I**'s activity is the **E** dimension subjective capacity. The continuity of this activity of **IE** is the subjective capacity of **O** dimension.

When **I** and **WI** first synchronize, the first expansion, the first lighting is the **A** sound rhythm. If there were no continuity of this initial synchronization, the expression of **A** would only be a spark — instantly extinguished. But the synchronization of **I** and **WI** is permanent, and that facet of the expression of the life dimension is the activity of **O** dimension. With this continuity, it becomes possible to divide and to judge. This activity is therefore the order of **I E O**.

The manifestation of the source of our life as the expression of life will and life power, from the a priori to the a posteriori world, occurs in the order of the Amatu Iwasaka sound chart: **I E O A U**. Because we are starting from the individual viewpoint, we see this order upside down: **U A O E I**. Iwasaka leads us back, step by step, to our own source, our native land.

If I attempt to explain this in the opposite direction, from the universal viewpoint, I am afraid it will only create more confusion. It is different when I can speak directly to a student. Readers of this book only have access to dead letters, which cannot hold the actual life rhythms. The written word is another mirror image, its reflection reverses the reader's viewpoint once again. It is all too easy to be misled by an explanation given in writing.

I have already explained my meaning in several different ways, but perhaps one more will make it clearer. In the Amatu Iwasaka sound chart, the order of mother dimensions shows first the subjective capacities of **U A O E** and then the subject itself, **I**. This representation was created to simplify the practicant's study. In reality, the action of the four dimensions' subjective capacities is a part of the activity of **I**, the life will. The action of the four subjective capacities is the action of the **I** dimension. There is no chronology, all the dimensions are expressed simultaneously with every second that passes.

The Amatu Iwasaka chart structures the mother dimensions into an order, but there is in fact no separation, no time, no space in the a priori world. The subjective capacities of all four dimensions appear at the same time in Naka-Ima, on the screen of our consciousness. All four spring into existence together. Their single source, **I-WI**, the pure and absolute subject, is behind each subjective capacity as that dimension's will and power.

I-WI is the desire and strength of each dimension. It is never manifested in its own right, it never appears to a posteriori human consciousness. We can only realize its four expressions, its four facets: the four mother dimensions.

This is why, without the Kototama Principle, it is impossible to find the source of our own life. It is like the story of the bluebird. The children look for it everywhere. They know it exists, but they can never find it. The Bluebird, like many other traditional children's stories and fairy tales, is another symbolic reference to the Kototama Principle.

THE RELATIONSHIP BETWEEN THE KOTOTAMA PRINCIPLE AND THE BIBLE

I n the first three chapters, I have outlined the Kototama Principle. As an explanation, it is far from complete, and the reader must not think that he has understood the principle of life simply because of what he has read here. I have searched for nearly thirty years, trying to grasp the content of Kototama Futomani. I have spent all my energy in this practice and I cannot say that I have yet completed it.

Years ago, through my study, I learned of the existence of the ancient documents I mentioned earlier. There are two different types of documents. The first relate to the Kototama Principle itself; the second are the history of the first, spiritual civilization.

These two treasures were secretly handed down from generation to generation in the country which has become Japan. Many other documents and relics, the world over, may yet come to light. What made the transmission easier in Japan was that the documents were kept in shrines, and were considered the property of Sumela Mikoto.

Sumela Mikoto is the highest of the god men, a human being who has completely grasped the Kototama Principle and who embodies the life will of the universe. In our modern era, this position was held symbolically by the Emperors of Japan. The ancient records became their property, and as such they were held to be sacred. The Takeuti family itself, guardians of the documents since they were hidden, is not yet allowed to open some of the jars in which they are buried.

The ancient world chronicles and the documents referring to the Kototama Principle were hidden separately. Only a few people in each generation knew of their existence; fewer yet studied their contents.

Until the end of the second world war, the Japanese Emperor was considered to be a living god: Alahito Kami. When Japan lost the war, the Emperor Hirohito stepped down from his position and announced: "I am a man". He resigned his divine position of his own free will and the place of Sumela Mikoto was left empty. The Takeuti Documents had belonged to the god-men. They could now be opened to ordinary people.

This may be difficult for Westerners to understand, particularly for the younger generations. But in terms of the correct ethical spirit, no one could touch the god-men's treasures until they no longer had an owner.

That is the visible event: the Takeuti Documents became accessible upon the Emperor's announcement that he was an ordinary man. But the decision to make this announcement was guided by the policy of Amatu Hitugi. It was a decision of **IE** dimension, made by the Emperor's own life will. The final choices and actions of all human beings are always determined by the human seed, the judgment of life. That is what I call the policy of Amatu Hitugi.

Moses was born, and filled the place recorded in the Old Testament — and the Old Testament itself was written. Jesus Christ came and performed his mission — and the New Testament was written. These events are not individual choices or creations. At bottom, Moses and Christ were obeying the will of Amatu Hitugi or the current of humanity as a whole. Great men embody this current at a given time, but they are not acting upon a personal decision.

Amatu Hitugi gives us the desire to work in a particular direction. That goal is what draws us on, it is what we are happy to do. It is, in other words, our mission. Moses and Christ did not care what passing pleasures they were throwing away, they had something to achieve and they could never have been happy if they had turned aside.

This is the way in which Amatu Hitugi guides us; this is what prompted Hirohito's announcement. His decision made it possible to open the secret documents, and particularly the Kototama Principle, to the public.

Kototama is the principle of human life, it is the totality of human capacity. Open it now, by Amatu Hitugi's order, and compare it with all the ancient texts of our civilization. Every sacred text, every ancient philosophy, the I Ching, the Bible, are symbolic explanations of the source of life.

Until yesterday, we could only study the symbols. Now we must look at their origin, at the reality of human life.

About ten thousand years ago, our ancestors started translating the principle of Kototama into symbols: mythology, iconography, numerology. We must now reverse this, re-translate these traditions and make their original meaning clear. That is the absolute order of Amatu Hitugi. It is the order behind the Emperor's words when he said: "I am not a god".

I am not sure whether the Japanese Emperor knew this or whether his was an unconscious action, forced, as he thought, by political circumstances. The result is the same. Consciously, or unconsciously, the policy of Amatu Hitugi guides the activity of human capacity.

From generation to generation, the current flows on and gathers momentum. Scientifically, we have gone from the abacus to the computer. Morally ... two generations ago, a divorce was a terrible shame. In Japan, schoolchildren would not have spoken to the child of divorced parents. Today, divorce is the norm.

The current leads us in the direction we must take. In our day, the process is accelerating as we reach the end of this particular expression. There have always been changes from generation to generation.

Three, four, five generations ago, children already disagreed with their parents, but there was always a respect for tradition. That is completely finished. It has become impossible to establish any structure, any discipline. Today, if one is not interested, one simply turns one's back and leaves. No one can accept anything which would curtail the fulfillment of their immediate desires. The material, scientific current has reached its fullest expression.

Sociologists and politicians look at the situation and say: "This is normal. Technology has unsettled our values, our culture has evolved too fast. But we have made great progress and in time, we will catch up with ourselves". But again, that is only a superficial viewpoint.

The evolution of a culture and its different side effects all follow the current of the human **I** dimension. The external evolution is only an expression of the flow of our inner dimensions, in one direction or another.

We can say that Einstein is the father of modern science, that Picasso initiated modern painting. It was in fact the **IE** dimension at the core of their being which put them in the forefront of their time. If they had failed, someone else would have come forward, because they were manifesting the expression of their time.

In the spring, **IE** dimension makes all the flowers come out in the right order, whatever the external circumstances.

I have already explained that the action of the eight father rhythms of **I**, the life will, is **E** dimension. It is the capacity of judgment.

The strength, the power of the **I** dimension is **WI**. **WI** is created by the final concentration of the total energy of the universe. Therefore, **I-WI** is always in perfect harmony, because it is the flow itself of the energy of the universe.

We say there are four seasons in a year. The **I-WI** dimension of human beings harmonizes with these changes; conditions are different according to the place in which we live. In Japan, the seasons are clearly divided, three months for each. In Europe, they are not nearly so clearly defined, and in tropical regions, there are only two seasons: the rains and the dry weather.

The people living in different regions synchronize and adapt to the changes of the seasons. But if it happens that the **I-WI** dimension in a human being cannot harmonize with outside conditions, that person dies. **I-WI** is life itself; if the body cannot follow, it is doomed. **I-WI** must synchronize; if the body cannot, they must part company. The **I-WI** dimension itself of course never dies, since it is universal energy itself.

The four dimensions of universal energy recognized by science (this is my point of view, and not an absolute knowledge), will also have four seasons. The world of the four a priori dimensions must also undergo a transformation cycle. If we represented their seasons' cycle as wave frequencies, their different expressions would shape different patterns, some more strongly marked, some less.

The cycle of an **U** dimension wave, whose expansion is the smallest, would in universal terms also be the shortest. It might perhaps span a century, while an **A** dimension cycle would take a thousand years to complete because it travels so much farther.

These cycles can also be pictured as segments of the great **I** dimension wave as it travels, without beginning or end, from the void to the void. An **I** dimension cycle can be said to be made up of interlocking segments, called by science gravitation, weak and strong interaction, electromagnetism. This is what my practice has shown me.

The scientific dimensions are limited. I don't know what science means by the terms it uses, but it has not understood the dimensions of life, from the galaxy to the least living cell. The energies detected in space by science cannot be equated with the mother dimensions.

Civilization, as the mirror of universal activity, must also have its waves and cycles. Peaks and valleys are expressed as social events. Individual humans, like Einstein or Picasso, take this expression upon themselves. They complete a part of the mission, but the mission exists beyond them.

Our present civilization began about ten thousand years ago. At first, it was only a trickle, but five thousand years later, the new current was being felt all over the world. Today, it has become irresistible.

Life cannot remain static. The current of our knowledge must change from generation to generation, but no individual invents a change. Changes are the expression of the fluctuations of the life dimension. These waves, rising and falling in the space of the universe, are expressed to the human life will judgment **IE** as inspiration. That is the manifestation of the policy of Amatu Hitugi. It is the order, the law of the activity of the universe as a whole. Religious people call this the law of God.

At the core of our physical life, our void center is guiding us and giving us our physical and spiritual capacities. It acts through **IE** dimension, the judgment of the life will. This cannot appear to us intellectually, through reasoning, but only as an inspiration. Inspiration is the highest level of our spiritual dimension; it is an absolute order from the source to the a posteriori human being. It is impossible for the a posteriori human capacity to go against this order.

This is true — but it is only true of the human being who is capable of hearing the orders of his own source. I am, unfortunately, speaking to a posteriori human beings of the present day, who have not yet opened the inner eye of **IE** dimension. They have this dimension in them but do not know it, and they live only through the desires of the four subjective capacities of **U A O E**. They expand all of their energies in these dimensions and believe they are complete human beings. But that is not yet true.

Humanity today does not hear the orders of the **IE** dimension. These orders cannot be heard, cannot be seen by the a posteriori physical capacity. If this capacity is all you have to guide you, you will unconsciously break the law of the universe — the law of God — every day of your life. Unconsciously or consciously: some have studied the life principle and still choose to put their individual desires first. These people know they are breaking the law.

The religious concept of divine retribution is a symbolic way of speaking of the permanent efforts every human must make, the perpetual jolts they suffer if they cannot hear the orders of the **IE** dimension. If you cannot harmonize your desire or your activity with the action of the **IE** dimension in you, you are perpetually working against yourself. If your day-to-day activity is not in harmony with the inner rhythm at the core of your being, you are permanently pulled in conflicting directions. **IE** is **IE**, and will go on being itself whatever you do. But in the stress created by your resistance, your physical or mental health will break down.

This is the cause of every illness, and it is also your "punishment". Why does everything seem to go wrong for some people? Why do others commit suicide when everything was apparently going so well? This is true of an individual's life, a family's, a nation's.

Once your equilibrium is destroyed — once you are sick — it becomes impossible to judge what is right or wrong. It is like the story of the three blind men describing an elephant. Each explored it with his hands as far as he could reach from where he was standing, and in turn said the elephant was: an enormous rough column with deep folds, a stringy hairy rope with a tuft at the end, a supple hollow tube. Each of them, as he felt the leg, the tail or the trunk, was absolutely convinced of having the entire truth. They believed what they personally were experiencing, without knowing that their capacity to experience the world was terribly limited.

When the individual's desires are put before his synchronization with the life dimension, it becomes necessary to establish and enforce laws. Our laws however are based on the same knowledge as our crimes. It only requires skill, money or power to escape the punishment of human law. But once a human being goes against the law of our creator — the **IE** dimension, the policy of Amatu Hitugi — no social position or power can help him. Every one is equal before that law. Every human has his exact punishment, according to the degree of his crime — because it is the punishment of his own inner self. His suffering is in direct relation with how far he has wrenched himself away from his own source.

The Hiding of the Kototama Principle

Kototama Futomani was hidden at the end of the first, spiritual civilization and the leaders of the world undertook to guide society toward the perfection of the second, materialistic and scientific civilization. This was the beginning of our present culture. According to the ancient records, it seems that this decision was made about ten thousand years ago. The actual hiding of the principle began to make itself felt perhaps eight thousand years ago.

The hidden documents referring to this are usually called the Takeuti Documents, because they are in the keeping of the Takeuti family. These documents, and various relics of the ancient time, are the treasures of the Koso Kotai Jingu, the oldest Shinto shrine of Japan. As I said earlier, the treasures of the shrine belonged originally to Sumela Mikoto. The Takeuti were the hereditary head priests, in charge of the Koso Kotai Jingu and of its secret documents.

A part of these documents are a chronicle of the events of Hinomoto Kuni. For example, the arrival of two brothers, Fu-I and Sin-no, is recorded. They came from China to study at the world center. They remained there for 36 years, studying the principles of the numbers 8 and 9 and their applications. When they returned to China, Fu-I created the I Ching and Sin-no laid down the basis of herbal medicine. This is recorded in great detail.

That is the first mention in the ancient records of teaching specifically the Kanagi and Sugaso principles. I will explain the content of these principles in the next chapter. This shows clearly that at the time it was written, the hiding of the Kototama Principle had already begun. Nowhere in the historical chronicles is there any mention of the principle of Amatu Futonolito — the full capacity of human life. It was no longer being taught to envoys from other lands.

In Hinomoto Kuni, the life principle was hidden much later than in the rest of the world. Or rather, it was hidden from the ordinary people but preserved in a few families. The process was completed by the first Sumela Mikoto of the Kami Yamato era. This is Jimmu, first Emperor of Japanese history as it is taught today. The older records being hidden, Jimmu has become a mythical figure, descended from the gods in the shadowy beginnings of history. He actually lived about 2,650 years ago — this being written in 1990.

The names of all the Sumela Mikoto, generation by generation, are listed in the Takeuti Documents. Their lives are recorded: where they traveled, what they did, what troubles they had in those times and where. The creations of each are given: alphabets, precepts of agriculture, cooking, and medicine.

Jimmu ordered the hiding of these records and of the relics of the ancient time, and began to import elements of the cultures of foreign countries: China, India, Korea. Modern history books call this the Jimmu revolution. Hinomoto's passage into the new era was continued by later Kami Yamato Emperors, but Jimmu began it. He effectively cut away the past, to the point where it is believed today that before his time — if he really existed — there were no letters, no history, no culture ... no Hinomoto Kuni.

When the decision to hide the Kototama Principle was made, emissaries were sent out from Hinomoto Kuni to develop separate cultures, different languages, different viewpoints throughout the world. Nationalism and individualism were encouraged, and the peoples of the world began to forget that there had ever been a central government. Finally, last of all, this change reached Hinomoto Kuni, and in Jimmu's time, the ancient world center began to import again what had been created elsewhere. Jimmu gave orders for Hinomoto Kuni, now becoming a country like any other, to be the cultural colony of China and India.

In spite of what is being taught today, letters did exist in Japan before the importation of Chinese characters. Some of the Takeuti Documents are written in the ancient Kami yo moji (moji meaning letters). But the written word did not hold the place it is given in modern society. People were not educated through books.

Letters are the representation of words, but they do not hold the rhythms of those words. That living rhythm only passes in the direct contact between teacher and student. An education based exclusively on the written word is like taking an Egyptian mummy and saying: "This is your ancestor". It is not true. It is only an empty husk.

All modern scholars believe that Japanese culture was imported entirely from other lands. I believed this too when I was young. When I began to understand the content of the Kototama Principle, I felt the need to find out more about the past. If everything in Japanese culture was imported, from where had the Kototama Principle come? But there was no trace of its having originated anywhere else, and I began to accept the ancient Takeuti chronicles and their version of history.

The importation of foreign cultures continued over the generations, and Temmu, the 41st Emperor of the Kami Yamato epoch (our present era) finished the Kojiki. Today, this is generally believed to be the oldest book in Japan and the beginning of the indigenous culture. By that time, the Kototama Principle was completely hidden, and the ancient world records buried in the Takeuti shrine.

The hiding of the past was very thorough. Modern historians are no longer sure Jimmu ever existed; the Kototama Principle has been translated into religious symbols. Originally, Ko Shinto was not a religion, it was Kototama. It is only when the principle was veiled that it became a religious dogma like the others.

The Kojiki is a sort of mythology, explaining the creation of the world. The sounds of Kototama Futomani are presented as gods and goddesses; their names are those of the Sumela Mikoto of ancient times.

The confusion is taken even further by the book's being written in Chinese Kanji characters. This was a brilliant way of veiling the original sense of the text. For example, "Kana" is the real sound, the actual life rhythm as spoken by the god-men. But if it is interpreted as meaning the word, or the name of god, and that meaning is the one written in Kanji characters, the original sense is completely lost. A pure sound is its own meaning, but in the symbolic Chinese characters, one sound can have a multitude of meanings. The way the sound is written completely alters its sense — and that altered sense is the one transmitted when the text is read.

The Kojiki was completed about the year 711 of our era. Like all mythologies, it tells of the loves and conflicts of the gods. They marry and have children: this symbolizes the synchronization of the eight father rhythms of **I** dimension with the mother sound rhythms, creating the child sounds and all phenomena.

The reason for hiding the Kototama Principle

If the Kototama Principle is the final truth of human life, why was it necessary to hide it? I will try to explain the reason.

The Kototama Principle is the principle of all the living beings in the world, it is the principle of life itself. After long years of searching and practice, I am completely sure of this. But all religious believers feel the same way. Not only religious people: artists, scientists, politicians and businessmen are all perfectly sure their way of approaching life is best.

The confidence of the Kototama practicant is not the same as that of other people: it is not a belief. Kototama is not an abstract concept, or a way of carving out a pleasant life for oneself in a difficult world. The ancestors who perfected this principle had no doubts, they knew this was the principle of life. The practicant who grasps the contents of the sounds sees clearly the manifestation of his own life, and of the life of the entire universe.

This civilization, based on the materialistic and scientific viewpoint, has spent eight thousand years in its search for the ultimate nature of matter. It has now reached the truth: after breaking matter down into smaller and smaller particles, it has found the void. But matter is only one dimension of universal capacity. Compared to this long study of what is accessible to the physical senses, who can say how long it took to grasp the complete contents of all the a priori dimensions? How many thousands of generations, how many people in each generation? Countless human beings, like my own teacher, Ogasawara Sensei, spending all their energy, all their life in the search for their own source.

Finally, 56,100 years ago, the Kototama Principle was perfected. The people who had perfected and grasped it were the natural leaders of the world. They were what I call god-men: men and women who had completely grasped the contents of the Kototama Principle, representatives of the universal law. They formed a court around Sumela Mikoto, the living embodiment of the judgment of the **IE** dimension. In accordance with the basic law regulating all human activity, they began to guide the development of civilization and culture all over the world.

From the time the principle was perfected until about ten thousand years ago, this type of development was carried on. In those days, the civilized societies leaned toward the spiritual rather than the material side. This was the era of the first civilization. As is said in the Old Testament, there was only one language, one nation on earth. The "world headquarters", where Sumela Mikoto resided when he was not on his travels, and where the god-men were educated, was Hinomoto Kuni.

It seems that the earth was rather different in that time. I am not an expert on these matters, but apparently, the area of the present day Japanese islands was still joined to the mainland.

About ten thousand years ago, the world leaders, particularly of the younger generation, began to ask for a change to be made. They were emissaries who had been sent to foreign lands. They had been sent to teach the life principle — but not everybody could reach their level. Very few people could grasp what they were trying to explain. Most students would only go a small way, many never understood even the rudiments of the principle.

Every human being has the same capacity — but not everyone has the same interest, or the same integrity in their research.

Society was at that time divided into two groups. There were the god-men and those who followed them, ordinary people who had not grasped the Kototama Principle for themselves but were willing to be guided by those who had. And there were the others who were only interested in gratifying their immediate desires. They wanted satisfaction on the personal, individual level; they wanted pleasant sensations for their physical or spiritual senses.

The god-men alone were capable of standing back and judging the origin of their desires; they followed the a priori universal life will. The others were only interested in its a posteriori manifestations, and if anyone else, even a god-man, got in the way of this satisfaction, they were capable of murder.

This lasted over forty thousand years. God-men and emissaries worked all over the world, and in spite of all their efforts, they could not create a completely peaceful society. The second group, who followed its selfish desires, always outnumbered the first.

Ordinary people simply could not see the point. Why spend so much time and energy listening to teachers, why go through such discipline, why go hungry, go without sleep, meditate ... . They listened to the god-men and they respected them, but they had no desire to search and grasp the principle for themselves. And so conflicts continued. Conflicts between individuals, conflicts between groups. It was possible to explain theoretically what freedom or harmony were, but ordinary people couldn't accept them if it meant curbing their immediate desires — on the spiritual or the physical side.

In the end, the younger leaders came before their elders saying: "We have worked for forty thousand years to make a perfect society, and we have not succeeded because the people cannot understand us. We follow the law, but they cannot. We have worked so hard for so long, and it has all been for nothing. Let us find another way.

We go to the people, we talk to them about the a priori world, but ordinary people want something they can see, hear, smell, touch. They must feel something with their senses before they will accept it."

The older leaders replied: "But you know as well as we do that the physical approach is only the satisfaction of the senses. The senses bring passing pleasures, but they cannot see the source of life. Their rule automatically sparks competition and violence. People have no respect for life when they are listening to their physical senses.

How will you build a perfect society from that? There would be no peace for anyone. It would be the sacrifice of everything on earth.

We cannot accept a road so completely opposed to the law of life. Of course, it is difficult to make ordinary people understand the Kototama Principle, but we can only go on as we have always done".

"Yes, we know this is the way of sacrifice. We understand that. Haven't we explained it to people ever since there were god-men? For forty thousand years, every generation has spent its entire life explaining it. What is the use of going on? There is still fighting and murder, they even come to kill us if what we say displeases them. This is already the sacrifice.

We try to show them the way to their own life, they kill us. How much longer must we go on? In the end, this will make a greater sacrifice than the development of a material civilization ever could.

Please, give us permission to guide society in this direction. If we cannot bring them to understand the activity of their senses, they must explore it for themselves. If we guide them straight to the mark, it can be done so much more quickly".

This discussion went on for a long time. Finally, the elder god-men agreed. They gave their consent, asking only that the work be begun as far away from Hinomoto Kuni as possible.

From my understanding of the Takeuti Documents, this discussion actually took place over a period of many years. It was finally decided to start the material civilization and from that point on, little by little, the references to the Kototama Principle are disguised.

Society had to be cut off from its source if it was to give itself wholeheartedly to the materialistic viewpoint. It also had to be able to find its way back when it decided that this viewpoint was not enough. Therefore, coded messages began to appear: mythologies, religions, philosophies. Their objective is to keep the spirit alive. Spirit is now opposed to matter and in competition with it, but the hints are there in the spiritual traditions, ready to be understood when the time comes and the key is uncovered once more.

Our society is clearly based on sacrifice. The earth is being destroyed. Human beings everywhere are suffering, mentally and physically. The ancient leaders saw very clearly how it would be for their descendants, and the elder god-men resisted this decision for a long time. Those who took the responsibility for this civilization knew they had to throw all their energies into their mission and finish it as quickly as possible. They had to reach the entire world, to guide every society in this direction. Every human being had to be drawn into this point of view.

This could never have been achieved if the Kototama Principle had remained in evidence. There would always have been people who chose the principle of life and resisted the materialistic current. The work would have taken longer, the destruction been even greater. It was necessary to hide the Kototama Principle. Hide it temporarily, for as short a time as possible, but hide it completely, so that no direct reference to it could be found on the face of the earth.

It could not be completely erased. Humanity must be able to find it again when we reached the end of the scientific civilization. Therefore it must be disguised, referred to indirectly, symbolized in a way that could be deciphered when the time came. This is the origin of all the world's religions.

From the oldest religions to Islam, the most recent, all dogmas symbolize the Kototama Principle. They provide a second pole for the duality, the opposition which is the basis of this civilization, and they keep alive a glimmer, a ghost of the truth for the people who are suffering through the scientific civilization.

At the very beginning of the spiritual civilization, when the Kototama Principle was first perfected, there were not many people on earth.

. Some of them began to understand and follow the law of the a priori life dimension. There was no conflict within these groups. The elders' word was absolute law for the younger: they knew their elders were speaking with the voice of life itself. The word of Sumela Mikoto met with absolute agreement. Without any material power, without armies or wealth, his word was as the word of God. The people who followed the Kototama Principle in that time are, I believe, the ancestors of the Celts.

The god-men were not born with an understanding of the Kototama Principle. In their first years, they were as misguided as any other children. But they were educated according to the principle, and those who grasped it were entrusted with the guidance of a foreign region. The nations of that time were not like modern countries with their frontiers and their laws. Kuni were natural divisions, according to the customs and ways of life suited to each geographical area. The only frontiers were natural. Different conditions required a different way of life — and that was the beginning of another Kuni.

The god-men created isolated centers in different lands and their teaching began to influence the world. The groups who followed the Kototama Principle formed peaceful societies, but they were a minority. Other groups could sometimes come to destroy what they had built. Sometimes, they were attacked directly, sometimes they were caught in the middle of a conflict which had nothing to do with them.

As time went on, humanity multiplied. Toward the end of the first civilization, the population had increased tremendously. With this came an increase in the human competitive sense. There was less and less vital space. As physical needs and desires became more difficult to satisfy, they became more important. The people began to say: "We are here, and our strongest desires are physical. Why should we resist them? I would do anything to get what I want."

This came about as naturally as the swelling of a river in the spring. We spoke earlier of the currents of universal life as the policy of Amatu Hitugi. To build a perfect civilization, humanity had to explore both ways: the spiritual and the physical. That is my understanding of the path humanity has taken.

All this is recorded in the Kojiki. The dispute between the gods Susano and Amaterasu is the conflict between the physical desires and the Kototama life dimension. Susano is a god, Amaterasu, a goddess. Susano symbolizes the Kanagi, Amaterasu, the Futonolito principle.

A perfect civilization is a civilization which satisfies both the spiritual and the physical sides. In our society, we are familiar with the violence of the physical viewpoint. It is just as foolish and violent to give expression only to the spiritual side and to try to tamp down the physical desires. Our physical desires exist, they are a part of us. We must at the very least calm them or we have no peace. We would not be complete humans without them. It is absurd to say that physical desires belong to a low dimension, or that they are dirty. Nothing in our nature is dirty. Without those desires, we would die.

It was necessary to explore the physical capacity and to perfect a material civilization. The younger leaders felt that they must guide society in accordance with this current. They recognized their own physical desires in those of their people.

The elder god-men had passed beyond those needs into the peace of their old age. They could remember physical pleasures, but they knew how ephemeral they were. The physical drive had left them, and they could no longer take it very seriously. They knew that pleasure was not happiness, and from their point of view, physical love was not worth all the trouble it caused. But the younger god-men could not see things in the same way. Their desires were still strong and vital, and it was unthinkable simply to disregard them in the name of a higher wisdom.

Many hundreds of years passed between the original request and the final agreement: "This is the way it must be". Such a reversal could not be instantaneous. It may be that some of the young leaders gave up hoping for the agreement of their elders and started the new mission on their own, in their own lands. At any rate, the sanction was finally given, and the change began to be felt in society.

This kind of revolution is a turning of the current of Amatu

Hitugi. How many centuries does it take to accomplish such a turning? We can only tell from the surface events of society. In our history, we have seen the gathering momentum of the materialistic viewpoint. Once the central world organization was dissolved, the political structures of the world were based on hereditary royalty. This was a memory, a pale approximation of the rule of the god-men: our kings ruled by divine right. This lasted for a long time, then was suddenly changed to a democratic policy on one side and a communistic system on the other. Less than a hundred years later, the communist form is collapsing, and the democratic is clearly showing its limitations. This is an example of the way in which society evolves. Naturally, the change from the spiritual to the material civilization was much slower.

The elder among the god-men could see that what the younger leaders said was true. They could also see that it was only the truth of the times, a temporary truth, and they wished to follow the eternal truth of universal life. It seemed to them at first that the young god-men gave too much importance to the truth of the lower dimensions. They knew that once the physical senses were given full sway, their greed must destroy everything in their paths. To go to the end of this viewpoint, humanity must destroy its environment and ruin every living thing, including the human body. They saw the sense of what the younger leaders wanted to do, but it was very difficult to accept.

"Every pebble is a part of your mental activity. If you destroy a single stone, you destroy a part of yourself. What you are asking leads to the corruption of human mental actions and emotional senses. How do you get back from there? From what can you build again peace of mind and a healthy environment?"

The younger god-men were also terribly saddened by the perspective opening before them, but they saw no other way. They felt the second civilization was a necessary thing, the road humanity must take.

The god-men finally came to an agreement, but their argument goes on inside each of us, at every moment. It reflects the two fundamental viewpoints of life. The older god-men were speaking from the **IE** life dimension, the judgment of the life will; the younger from the **AE** or **UE** dimensions.

As they became older, and completely opened the eye of their life will, the god-men could see their own bodies as phenomena of the **WA** dimension. In **U**, there is no subject, no object. **WA** is the light of life, the creation of life. Science cannot see beyond **WA** and so believes it is the subject. A scientist is a **WA** phenomenon, looking outward at other **WA** phenomena. This viewpoint is the basis of modern civilization.

In this discussion, the young leaders were the representatives of the desires of the ordinary people — the people who could not enter into the way of Kototama. The discussion itself, like the agreement finally reached with the older leaders, was also a reflection of the policy of Amatu Hitugi.

When they agreed, the elder god-men did so upon certain conditions. They would follow the new civilization. But since, as they all knew, they were going toward great sacrifices and great crimes, this decision could only be temporary. The new civilization must be completed as soon as possible and as soon as it was complete, that very day, humanity must be guided back to the Kototama Principle. The young leaders, with their whole heart, accepted these conditions.

All the great spiritual leaders like Christ and Buddha have said: "I am going to sleep, but when the time comes, I will return. I will seem to die and one day I will rise from the dead". These leaders were all missionaries of the second civilization, and their words are based on the Kototama Principle. Humanity had to turn aside from the complete truth of life to explore the world of material phenomena. They were promising that the principle of life would return.

The younger god-men, with the support of the elder, began the work of hiding the principle. Many of them gave different symbolic explanations of the creation of life, and nation after nation adopted them and based their cultures on them. Each time, the fifty sounds of the **IE** dimension were presented differently but each time, the code was clear enough to be decrypted when the time came.

The elder members of the god-men's assembly asked for the change to begin as far away as possible. Hinomoto Kuni had to remain a center of education. As long as emissaries should be needed, it was necessary that one place on earth hold the original principle and educate the leaders of the new epoch. This is my understanding, based on the study of the ancient Takeuti Documents and of the Kojiki, and on comparing them with the Kototama Principle.

It is not easy for the people of the second civilization to

understand what the world was like in the first, spiritual era. There were no separate countries as we understand them — that concept could only exist in our civilization. After the decision to follow the materialistic way was made, separations and frontiers slowly came into being. They only came to mean what they mean today, about 3,000 years ago.

In the ancient documents, the names of kings of different countries — kuni — are mentioned. The original meaning of "kuni" was a geographical area, and also the people who lived there. A nation was a group of people living in a particular way, suited to the region in which it was settled.

In the Takeuti chronicles, it is recorded that in the 22nd generation of the Kami Yamato era (our modern era), the original letters were changed to Chinese characters by Ryu Ryaku. From that time on, the term "kuni", written in Chinese letters, took on the foreign concept and came to mean "country" in the present sense of the word.

The nations are presented in the ancient documents as belonging to five racial colors: red, yellow, white, blue and black. Again, this notion of races did not carry the same sense as it does today. There was no sense of hierarchy, of higher or lower races — no suspicion based on the color of the skin.

With the mixing that occurred over the millennia, the modern races are not exactly the same as those of ancient times. The intermingling seems to have been closest between the white, blue and red colors, which are no longer as clearly separated as the yellow and black. The blue race only seems to remain as a color of the eyes — or perhaps in very pale white skins which have a slight blue tinge.

The god-men or leaders of the first civilization were educated in the world center, in Hinomoto Kuni. Some remained there, and some were sent to other lands. The latter seem to have created smaller centers, branches of the great center in Hinomoto Kuni. The god-men in those branches were in close contact with the peoples surrounding them. When the second civilization began, these branches became the great political centers: China, East India, Egypt, Rome, Central America (Yucatan), and Greece.

Some of the god-men sent out as emissaries settled in one area, others traveled from branch to branch. These were often specialists in one discipline; agriculture or medicine for example, which they taught wherever they went. Almost all the god-men, even those who had taken the responsibility for a specific region, traveled a great deal.

Greatest of the god-men was Sumela Mikoto. The man or woman who held this position was elected; but again, the term held a very different meaning in that time. There was no question of campaigning, or of trying to win over or influence anyone. The god-men knew each other's capacities completely. They discussed the question together, and their decision had to be unanimous. Today, the election of the Pope still requires all the voices of the assembly, but that is the only resemblance between his election and that of Sumela Mikoto.

Sumela Mikoto resided in Hinomoto Kuni, but traveled all over the world. As he or she guided society, it seems to have been necessary to visit the different branches and to make contacts with the kings of different nations.

The journeys, visits and achievements of Sumela Mikoto are recorded in the Takeuti Documents. Some went to Europe, some to the Americas, some to Asia... . They always traveled with a following of several hundred people; generally teachers of or specialists in a specific discipline. As they visited different places, Sumela Mikoto would ask some of them to remain. In some cases, the people of a kuni asked Sumela Mikoto for a leader, and he appointed one from his retinue.

There was always a close connection between each branch and the world center. The god-men exchanged visits, and went to Hinomoto Kuni to pay their respects to Sumela Mikoto. They also sent young people there to be trained as future leaders. Each important branch would surround itself with smaller centers. These satellites were not necessarily in the charge of a god-man: there were also lesser leaders with the title of king. Once again, there is a survival of this in the Pope-appointed kings of the past, or in the idea that kings hold their position by divine right.

When the second civilization began, the first idea of these kings was to overthrow the god-men who had appointed them, and to take their places. They began to fight among themselves to conquer each other's territories.

The Takeuti Documents record that the islands of Miyoi and Tami Alai (Mu and Atlantis) sank into the sea. There were important branches on both islands, entrusted to groups of god-men.

When I re-read the preceding passage, it did not seem sufficiently clear, and I would like to add a few more explanations.

I wrote that the change from the first to the second civilization was made at the request of the younger generation of god-men. This could be interpreted as meaning that the desires of the ordinary people had dictated their decision. This is not the order in which it happened.

I explained that during the first civilization, the world was divided into different kuni, each with a spiritual leader with the title of king. These leaders were named either by Sumela Mikoto or by the god-man of the closest branch, and they were responsible for the policy of the area they represented. The god-men in charge of foreign branches made frequent visits to the surrounding kuni. They were the teachers and guides of these regions. They knew the situation and the problems of each, and they were very close to their peoples. It would seem to us now that such a society could have been guided according to the law of life and made perfectly peaceful. But that is not what happened.

This social structure was based on the Kototama Principle. Within a communist country, the people actually convinced that communism is the best possible way of life are few, just as in democracies, very few people actually agree with the government. In the first civilization, the people who actually practiced the Kototama Principle were a minority. Some local leaders were educated according to the principle, and had some understanding of it. In other areas, there was no education, no civilization — the people were primitive and their way of life was no different from that of animals.

As a parenthesis, I would like to say that Darwin's theory of mankind's descent from the apes is much too simplistic. Primitive human bones cannot be compared to modern human bones (or for that matter the bones of ancient and modern apes) to draw any certain conclusions. The climate, the environment, the way of life and the food eaten in ancient times were all completely different from ours. The bones of the living beings of those days had to be different from ours, and science cannot judge which could have belonged to human beings, and which to apes.

The difference between a human being and an ape is in the content of their physical manifestation. The capacity of their mother dimensions is not the same. It is impossible to determine this content from the external appearance of bones long dead.

The modern knowledge of the way people lived in those early ages is based on this same viewpoint, applied to history or archaeology. On external evidence, researchers define our ancestors as primitive, uncivilized people. We define civilization as the creation of great buildings, technology, science. It is true that our ancestors' civilization was not oriented toward material creations, but it is a mistake to say that they were not civilized at all. Modern people feel that our civilization is a vast improvement over the "pre-historic" way of life. But we have no notion of what that life was, and what we call history is only the chronicling of the second, materialistic civilization.

In the times of Moses and Buddha and in their countries, the people had none of the comforts of modern times. Almost every one walked barefoot and fought with swords.

In Mahomet's time, technology had not developed much further. But in the ancient time of those uncivilized cultures, our ancestors practiced and taught the Kototama Principle.

Modern times are ruled by the twin viewpoints of religion and science. We build magnificent churches, and people devote their entire lives to praying in them from dawn to dusk. Religion and science only differ in the symbols they use; both are expressions of our civilization. Why do we not make shrines dedicated to the Wright brothers or to Einstein, the inventor of the atomic bomb? Modern people should reflect more seriously on their own contradictions.

I explained earlier that the first civilization comprised two groups: the god-men and their structured societies, and those outside the structure who lived only for the day to day fulfillment of their natural desires. This second group really was primitive and created endless difficulties for the first. They stole from them, they attacked them. The cultured people attempted to educate them, but they were not interested. All their acts were geared toward the satisfaction of their physical needs. They could not conceive that there was more to life; all they cared for was to survive another day as safely as possible.

The civilized people led by the god-men did their best to teach them language, letters, and the rudiments of culture. It became possible in some cases to communicate with them. The content of their knowledge opened out more widely but their basic impulses were still based on the desires of **U** dimension. The force that drove them was greed, especially for food. This attitude does not belong only to those times. The well-educated people of our day are driven by the identical impulse. As time goes on, it becomes more and more obvious that greed controls the life of our society.

At the end of the first civilization, these desires and ideas spread with the increase of the world's population and the human mentality came to be controlled by **U** dimension. The world leaders, in daily contact with the ordinary people, understood that it was impossible to control this trend through the counter-influence of the Kototama Principle. The kings they had trained were using their superior knowledge to gain advantage or to feed their pride. What was happening was a terrible deterioration of the human spirit, it went against the highest dimensions of life, but the god-men had to admit it as a reality. The world's civilization was spontaneously going in this direction, and civilization is a mirror of the activity of the universe.

They discussed it on the local level and saw that they must accept it as a decision by Amatu Hitsugi. The Kototama Principle must be veiled. They must follow the current, encourage it, and try to perfect it so as to return to the truth of life as soon as possible. It was then that the young god-men first brought their request before the assembly in Hinomoto Kuni.

This is my understanding, reached through the study of the ancient documents and the practice of the Kototama Principle. It may be that my vision is not entirely accurate, but the records of the days of our ancestors, on the whole, are. If there is a mistake, it lies in my personal interpretation.

The ancient documents of Japan

Modern Japanese scholars hold that before the year 711, when the Kojiki was completed, Japanese culture had produced no books. Actually, there exist many documents written in the traditional letters. These letters are called Kami Yo moji, the letters of the era of the gods.

Some of the texts written in these characters were translated into Chinese Kanji characters. Some are written in a mixture of Kanji and Kami Yo moji, and translated into the modern Japanese language. Almost all of these documents and relics date from the last ten thousand years, after the decision to hide the Kototama Principle. In these documents, the principle is already symbolized in the names and actions of the gods.

The fifty sounds of Kototama Futomani were not handed down directly as the contents of the Principle. They were trans-

mitted from generation to generation as the Yamato language —
the origin of the modern Japanese language. The Principle itself
was very strictly hidden, surviving only in documents held by a
few ancient families — the Imperial family among them. Today,
it has become almost impossible to find any documents referring
directly to the Kototama sound principle, but the chart of the fifty
sounds, in the order of Amatu Kanagi is studied daily by all
Japanese schoolchildren as their "alphabet".

The traces of the life principle which can be found today in
Japan's ancient documents are almost always allusive. They are
generally expressed in religious terms. These, along with the
ancient historical chronicles which are, as I said before, an entirely separate body of documents, are the symbolized aspect of the
Principle.

I have unfortunately never studied the ancient Kami Yo characters, and cannot read the documents written in these letters. I
was lucky enough however to study the Kototama Principle itself
with a real master: Koji Ogasawara Sensei.

A little over 100 years ago, Meiji, great grandfather of the present Emperor of Japan, revolutionized the life of his country. For
centuries, Japan had been ruled by warriors and the Emperor had
become a powerless ceremonial figure. Meiji took back the reins
of government into his own hands and started importing the ways
of the Western world into Japan. It was he who initiated the entry
of Japan into modern times.

Meiji married a daughter of one of the oldest families of
Japan, the Fujiwara. The custom in ancient families is for a
daughter, upon her marriage, to bring a dowry to her husband.
This lady was marrying the Emperor, and the dowry had to be the
family's most treasured possession. The new Empress brought
with her an extremely secret document, containing the key making it possible to decipher the Kojiki and to re-translate it into the
original life principle. The Fujiwara document was only a frag-
ment — but its other half had been handed down the generations... in the Emperors' family.

When the two parts were joined, Meiji and the Empress began
the enormous task of "translating" the Kojiki into its original
meaning. They asked a third person to join them: Harumichi
Yamakoshi Sensei, the royal family's professor of calligraphy and
an expert on ancient documents.

Theirs was a very long and very difficult undertaking. The

three original students died, but the work was continued by Hakimasa Yamakoshi Sensei, son of Harumichi Yamakoshi, and, like him, a professor of calligraphy. Koji Ogasawara, my master, was the secretary of the second Yamakoshi Sensei. He worked with him in the deciphering of the Kojiki, wrote out his notes, and became committed in his turn to the recovery of the ancient meaning of the book. It was he who completed and published the translation after the death of Hakimasa Yamakoshi Sensei. The title of the completed work is "The Hundred Deities of Kototama", and it was printed in Japan, on the first of June 1969.

I started studying with Ogasawara Sensei in 1963, before the publication of his book. I had already practiced the Kototama Principle in its symbolic form with Ueshiba Sensei, the founder of Aiki-do. Thanks to him, my interest in the Principle was already strongly rooted.

When Ueshiba Sensei died, I was teaching Aiki-do in France as a representative of the Tokyo Aiki-Kai. Unbelievable things suddenly began to happen to me during the courses — bursts of superhuman power. The first few times took me completely by surprise. One day, as I was facing my students, one of the tatami mats behind me was lifted a foot into the air. The mats in that hall were tightly wedged together, it was an enormous surface and it had been secured with a frame to prevent the mats from slipping. Two of my students jumped to their feet and tried to push it down. One of them jumped up on it, and a violent jar almost threw him off again. He knelt and pressed it down with his hands — and the mat slid smoothly back in its place.

Still in France, in a dojo in Annecy, a great gymnasium lamp, hanging thirty feet above me, burst when I lifted my hand with a kiai. In London, the same thing happened with a glass cupola in the roof. In other seminars, an enormous blackboard bolted to the wall fell, the iron rod holding the dressing room curtain crashed down. I came to recognize the feeling which came before these explosions. I knew that something was going to happen, but I had absolutely no control over it. I would project my ki energy in an exercise, and inanimate objects would leap from their moorings or burst apart.

This was extraordinary, but extremely unpleasant. It was not the power of life but a violent, destructive power — something like the power of the atomic bomb. I spent hour upon hour in meditation to try to understand what was happening, and I finally saw it: the spirit of Ueshiba Sensei was trying to come into me.

It was a legacy I could not accept. That enormous, violent martial power did not lead the way I wanted to go. For seven days, I prayed as humbly as I could: "I am sorry but I cannot accept this. Please forgive me, please understand that this is not the way for me". At last a heavy weight was lifted from me. I felt as if I was free again.

It took me a little while to dare an experiment. I remembered very well the feeling I had before each incident. I re-created it as closely as I could, and projected all my power with a kiai. Nothing happened, and nothing of the sort has ever happened again. A few days later, I was put in contact with Ogasawara Sensei.

I learned much later that Ueshiba Sensei and Ogasawara Sensei had met ten years before. Sensei Ueshiba was the elder by about twenty years. He was very happy to meet another Kototama practicant. He told my teacher that he himself could not study or teach the theory of the life principle: his way of practice was the martial arts. But he, Ogasawara Sensei, could and must take the responsibility for that side.

I believe that when I said I could not receive the power he was offering me, Sensei Ueshiba sent me to Sensei Ogasawara.

From 2,650 years ago to the Meiji revolution 125 years ago, the Kototama Principle was completely hidden, even in Japan. In 711 AD, the Kojiki was completed, explaining the Principle in terms of the actions and interactions of gods and goddesses. The Principle began to be revealed again through the work of the three generations I have spoken of: the Emperor Meiji, his Empress and Harumichi Yamakoshi Sensei; his son Hakimasa Yamakoshi Sensei; and my master Koji Ogasawara Sensei.

The first three worked as pure scholars, without attempting to communicate their findings to anyone. The second Yamakoshi Sensei may have begun to teach, but it was Ogasawara Sensei who truly opened up the principle. He gave talks, published his books, and accepted students. Many people came to listen to him, but it seems now as if none of them truly took the principle as the guide for their lives. I lost contact with the Japanese practicants after Sensei Ogasawara's death.

These three generations completed the deciphering of the Kojiki. I personally feel no need to search for the same thing in other ancient books. In each, the truth of human life has been expressed in a different set of symbols. The source of human capacity and the origin of every aspect of the present civilization is fully explained in each. They are all important textbooks for students of Kototama, but the real understanding of the principle only comes through practice. To go further in the understanding of the Kototama Principle, it is not enough to study the ancient books. It is necessary to search inside and to awaken the content of the life dimension.

The historical records dating from the earliest times of our civilization are in a way not as reliable as the religious books. The sacred contents of the latter have often preserved them from change.

The historical chronicles date from different periods. Many only relate the history of one region, without placing it in relation to the rest of the world. Others are half-sacred, half-historical, and it is difficult to tell which parts belong to which category. In the process of veiling the Kototama Principle, they speak of actual people as deities, or symbolize the activity of the life principle as the acts of actual people. After repeated transcriptions and translations, it is almost impossible for modern historians to decide which passages are to be taken literally, which are to be taken as symbols, and which result from a simple error of interpretation by a long-ago translator. Without the reference of the Principle to help them, historians and archaeologists prefer to disregard these documents completely. They will not even consider the possibility that they might be actual historical records. As a result, young people never hear about them in school.

The Takeuti documents represent an enormous mine of information, but their age is so great that experts simply cannot accept them as authentic. They are the history of the world before the dawn of our civilization.

I agree that much of the text has been garbled, but I have confronted these documents with the Kototama Principle and with the mythologies and religions of the world, and the relationship is clear. I am certain that they are neither fairy tales nor forgeries.

Recognized histories all date from a much later era. As I have said before, they have all been tampered with in the interest of individual leaders or dynasties. There is no such thing as a completely accurate history book, and this of course is also true of the Takeuti documents. Ryu Ryaku, second Emperor of the Kami Yamato era, gave orders to Matori Takeuti, then head of the family and chief priest of the Koso Kotai Jingu, to translate some of the documents in his care from the Kami Yo moji to the Chinese characters. Such a translation is far from easy and it is probable that at that time some errors found their way into the finished work. Deliberate mistakes were certainly made in other instances for the sake of veiling the Kototama Principle.

The Kami Yo moji expressed pure sounds, each with its innate meaning. One letter referred to one sound. The Chinese characters express an abstract concept, a meaning rather than a sound. The single sound **TA**, for example, can in the Chinese characters be written in several different ways, all of which express different ideas. In the process of translation, mistakes were inevitable.

In some documents, there are places where words have visibly been crossed out. Sentences are incomplete, words are missing and phrases have been added, expressing a later interpretation or an individual comment. It is impossible for me to make an evaluation of the accuracy of each document, but the general impression of the whole is correct. I can accept it and agree with it.

If the Takeuti documents are read intellectually, detail by detail, the result is utter confusion. But the progression they show, and the general facts — this Sumela Mikoto traveled to such and such a land with this number of followers — those are the truth.

When I speak of ancient events, my reference is the Takeuti records. I first wrote about these documents in 1975. That year, with the permission of the Takeuti family, I chose excerpts of particular interest to Westerners and translated them into English. I would like to reproduce this translation here.

Translations from the Takeuti Documents

Introduction

The ancient historical documents existing in Japan are the legacy of an ancient age. The Japanese call them Shinto Kobunken, but they have nothing to do with the Shinto religion. They record the way in which our ancestors tried to organize the world into a peaceful society, a single nation speaking a single language. Their system of government was based upon the Kototama Principle.

These documents explain that the world government was centralized in the area which has become the modern country of

Japan. Because of the modern sense of national pride, and because the age of these documents is incredible in the light of conventional history, the Shinto Kobunken have yet to be seriously studied by official organizations.

In every epoch of our civilization, there have been groups or isolated individuals who tried to preserve the true history of the world and to hand it down to succeeding generations. There have also always been people who tried to grasp the reality of life. Both, in different ways, were going against the current of their times. I believe these people still exist in the world today and it is for them, to help them in their search, that I want to write about these documents.

I am not a scholar of ancient history. To avoid creating even more confusion, I have not added my own viewpoint, but translated from the ancient records word for word. This little book is written in the hope of informing today's society of the existence of these and other hidden records of our past.

No one can say that the history they were taught is absolutely accurate. The writers of history are sometimes biased, and not all the leaders of the past have cared to leave their particular errors on record. Parts of history have been erased for political reasons, and parts have been destroyed in different upheavals: invasions or natural catastrophes.

Whatever the pressures of the times, secret records were kept by people who lived outside the mainstream of society. They were sometimes persecuted, they generally had to hide or disguise their activities. In different ways, they suffered to preserve the truth. Not all the records kept in this way have come to light as yet, but one day, we can hope to have a complete picture of the history of the world before our civilization began.

Modern researchers can only go back three or four thousand years before reaching a point of non-comprehension in the face of what tradition tells them. But there is a key, and it can unlock the secrets of all the ancient mythologies, philosophies and traditions. Throughout the world, there are records of the ancient society of our ancestors. They have not yet been found, or not yet been recognized as historical accounts. They began to be hidden away eight to ten thousand years ago.

In that country, the ancient documents became a part of the treasure of the shrines. As sacred objects, they were considered to be the property of the Emperor, and no one was allowed to touch them. By far the greatest body of documents is kept in the Koso Kotai Jingu, the oldest shrine in Japan. This shrine, and its treasure, have been in the care of the Takeuti family for thousands of years. Many members of the family have given their lives for its protection, and over the centuries, the Koso Kotai Jingu relics have come to be known as the Takeuti documents.

The reason the ancient records were hidden is the same as the reason the Kototama Principle itself was hidden: to allow for the development of our modern civilization. This development was planned by the leaders of the ancient society — the Sumela Mikoto — and it was arranged that, at the end of this civilization, the hidden documents would surface to help guide the world's society into the next stage of its development. This has already begun.

The Takeuti documents are in three parts: the Book of Heaven, the Book of Earth, and the Book of Man. They give an account of the creation of heaven and earth, and of the beginning of the first civilization. The first Sumela Mikoto is named, and from that time, the travels and achievements of each succeeding generation of world leaders is minutely recorded. We are told of the histories of the different races, of the origins of the different languages, of the creation of the first alphabets. Over two hundred different alphabets are shown in the Takeuti documents, from which the Greek, Egyptian, Sumerian, Sanskrit and Chinese Kittan letters evolved.

There is information in these records about forgotten cultures, mentioned in no other chronicles. Many obscure fragments of the records we do have could be clarified by the Takeuti documents.

Also chronicled are the relations of the Sumela Mikoto with kings and leaders throughout the world. The Sumela Mikoto in person or one of his or her emissaries appointed the kings of the first civilization. Sumela Mikoto was the highest of the world leaders. The documents refer to Sumela Mikoto as a god-man, but they clearly indicate that both men and women were chosen for this position.

Until about four thousand years ago, there were no countries, no frontiers as we understand them today. The peoples of the earth were differentiated only by the five colors of race: black, blue, red, white and yellow. It is explained in the Takeuti documents that the first Sumela Mikoto of the Kami Yo era is the source of the five colors or races of humanity. This can probably be understood to mean

65

that the current of life, personalized by Sumela Mikoto, manifested the five races in that time. It is also said that in the year 686,608,621 of his reign, the second Sumela Mikoto parented princes and princesses of the five colors. This does not necessarily mean that Sumela Mikoto was their biological parent. Spiritual descent, the relation of teacher to pupil is also a way of giving life.

The center of the first civilization, located in the area of Japan, was the place where the leaders of society were educated, and the place of residence of Sumela Mikoto. Around Sumela Mikoto was an assembly of leaders. Students from all over the world would come to them to study the guiding principle of Kototama. If they managed to grasp it fully, they would be sent out in their turn as teachers and guides. Sumela Mikoto also traveled a great deal, going where his guidance was needed. Many Sumela Mikoto died on their travels and were buried in far away places.

The world center is referred to in the documents as Amatu Kuni or heaven country, Kamitu Kuni or the country of the gods, Hinomoto Kuni or the country of the source of the spirit, and Takamahala, the field of heaven. In other ancient texts, it is called the country of the East, or the country of the Messiah.

There still remains clear evidence of the great upheavals which changed the face of the earth. During one of the greatest, Mu and Atlantis sank into the sea. This event is recorded as having occurred during the month of May, in the 33rd year of the reign of the 69th Sumela Mikoto of the Fuki Aizu Tyo.

Geologists know that the earth repeatedly became like a molten ocean. This is shown by erosion patterns and by the presence of sea shells in the rocks of high mountains. In the ancient texts, this is recorded as having occurred during the sixth generation of Amatu Kami.

In that same reign, on March 26th of the year 200, Moze (or Moses) arrived at the world center. He studied there for twelve years, received the title of king from Sumela Mikoto, and was ordered to guide society into the material, scientific civilization.

Four generations later, Hinomoto Kuni entered into the modern age or Kami Yamato era. The 73rd Sumela Mikoto of the Fuki Aizu era decreed this change and became the first of the Kami Yamato era under the name of Jimmu Tenno — Emperor Jimmu. Jimmu is remembered today as a half-mythical figure, descended from the gods and founder of the dynasty of the Emperors of Japan. At this point, the hiding of the Kototama Principle is completed, the past of Hinomoto Kuni is forgotten, and the history of the modern country of Japan begins.

The Imperial family alone remembered the life principle, but their grasp of it was not what it had been. By the time the Kojiki was completed, even they had lost the capacity of god-men.

Until the 72nd generation of Fuki Aizu Tyo, Sumela Mikoto had guided the world's affairs in person. The 72nd Sumela Mikoto did not travel as his predecessors had done; the record does not say very much about him. With the 73rd generation and what is known in history books as the "Jimmu revolution", all traveling, all contact with the outside world ceased. Hinomoto Kuni had become a country like any other.

The Takeuti documents are not the only records of the ancient past in Japan. There are also the Toyoasihala Shinpu Waki, the Jyofuku Den, the Uyetu Fumi, the Kuki, Abe, and Mononobe documents. The Takeuti documents are however the largest and most important by far.

Japanese people today believe what they are taught in school: that the Kojiki and Nihon Shoki are the first books written in Japan; that before the importation of Chinese characters the Japanese people had no knowledge of the written word; that all Japanese culture was imported from China and India. The documents listed above show clearly that this is not true. The writer of the Kojiki himself, Futono Yasumalo, says in his introduction that there are documents written in letters symbolizing Kana (the word of god). These letters are the Kana moji or Kami Yo moji: "to arrive at their true meaning is both difficult and delicate". Modern scholars prefer to ignore this, as it would require a revision of every accepted idea of the past. They prefer to hold on to their knowledge — and to their positions.

The older documents indicate that the Kojiki and Nihon Shoki are symbolic explanations of the Kototama Principle, written by the order of Sumela Mikoto. These books appear to be chronicles of the past, but they belong to our era, in which the real past of humanity is hidden. The history of humanity can only be found in the Takeuti and other ancient texts. As I explained earlier, alterations and mis-translations have found their way into the oldest documents, and it has become difficult to discern their original meaning. But with an understanding of the Kototama Principle, it is possible to interpret them and to see how accurate they really are.

In my explanation of the Kototama Principle, I have stated that it is the source of all the religions, mythologies and philosophies of the world. The proof of this too can only be found in the Takeuti documents and in other ancient texts.

These documents record that Moses, Fu-I, Lao-Tsu and many others came to the world center to study and practice in the court of Sumela Mikoto. They each received from him a title and a mission and went to the lands he appointed for them. When the ancient documents are confronted with the Kototama Principle, it is possible to see the truth of those facts.

A few years ago, I met a historian to whom I showed a photograph of a drawing found among the Takeuti documents. I gave him no explanation, and asked him who he believed this drawing represented. I should add that this man was also a Freemason, and had access to traditions which an ordinary historian would not have known. He studied the reproduction of the drawing very carefully, took notes and measurements, detailed the different tokens depicted, and finally said that this was a drawing of Christ at the time of his return from his first voyage. This satisfied me, and I told him the real story of the life of Christ. I may add that it surprised him a great deal.

Many people will dismiss outright the possibility of Christ's journey to Hinomoto Kuni. They will argue that no one could have traveled such distances in the ships of those days. That is only our modern arrogance. The ancient documents clearly say that ships of the sea, ships of the air and ships of heaven (probably space ships) were being used as means of transportation in days even more remote.

In their explanation of the origin of life given in the Takeuti documents, the first god or creator of the universe is variously named Namumo, Aamin, Nonno, Naamo, Kaminagala, Meshia, Mumeshia. The first Sumela Mikoto is represented as being the direct descendant of this god.

I have already explained that the Sumela Mikoto guided the first civilization until about ten thousand years ago, when the decision was made to hide the principle and to guide the world onto the path of the scientific civilization. After the principle was hidden, the office of Sumela Mikoto was filled by a symbolic god-man, the Tenno (or Japanese Emperor).

From this point on, I have transcribed actual excerpts from the Takeuti documents.

The ancient documents divide the first civilization into the following eras, each of which is defined by the number or generations of Sumela Mikoto:

Amatu Kami era

7 generations, the seventh being divided into two parts.

Kami Yo era

This era counts 25 generations, each divided into a certain number of sub-generations. All the sub-generations bear the same name as Sumela Mikoto. It is not clear whether these were successive generations, or whether the god-men scattered over the earth at a given time are defined as so many "generations". Each god-man could at that time have taken the name of the reigning Sumela Mikoto.

1st generation	21 sub-generations
2nd generation	33 sub-generations
3rd generation	24 sub-generations
4th generation	22 sub-generations
5th generation	22 sub-generations
6th generation	22 sub-generations
7th generation	21 sub-generations
8th generation	20 sub-generations
9th generation	22 sub-generations
10th generation	20 sub-generations
11th generation	20 sub-generations
12th generation	18 sub-generations
13th generation	19 sub-generations
14th generation	22 sub-generations
15th generation	18 sub-generations
16th generation	16 sub-generations
17th generation	11 sub-generations
18th generation	10 sub-generations
19th generation	15 sub-generations
20th generation	13 sub-generations
21th generation	16 sub-generations
22th generation	11 sub-generations
23th generation	7 sub-generations
24th generation	5 sub-generations
25th generation	8 sub-generations

Fuki Aizu Tyo

73 generations, the 73rd becoming the first of the:

Kami Yamato Tyo

The present Emperor of Japan represents the 126th generation of this era.

Presentation

The Takeuti documents seem to give an explanation of the creation of the universe through our human recognition. In the fifth generation of the Amatu Kami era, god is created by the word. The order of our human manifestation and realization of universal life is explained. Letters are said to appear at this time. All the natural phenomena are explained and each given a god's name, and the transformations of natural phenomena are attributed to their respective gods. This is why the texts are very difficult to understand without the key of the Kototama Principle.

During the Amatu Kami epoch, divisions of time were established, very close to the divisions we use today: one revolution of the earth to one day, 30 days to a month, 12 months and 360 days in the year. The month was divided into three parts according to the phases of the moon. The first cycle of ten days was called Tate toka, the second Mado toka, and the third Komoli toka. The months were named as follows:

Mutuhi tuki	January
Kesali tuki	February
Iyayo tuki	March
Ubeko tuki	April
Sanaye tuki	May
Minatu tuki	June
Fukumi tuki	July
Hayale tuki	August
Nayona tuki	September
Kaname tuki	October
Sibulu tuki	November
Sihatu tuki	December

For example, during the first part of the seventh generation of the Amatu Kami era, the shortest day of the year was called Kone no kule, and occurred in Sihatu, Komoli toka, Kulehi (the last day).

The sunrise of the next day was the beginning of the New Year, Mutuhi tate, and was the festival day of Konome Halu (spring). The four seasons were:

Konome Halu	Spring
Kuni Atu	Summer
Tanatu Aki	Fall
Koneno Fuyu	Winter

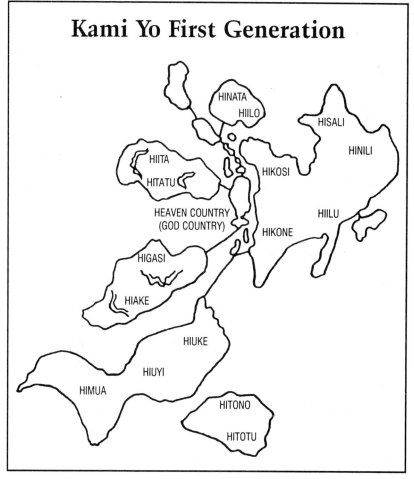

Kami Yo First Generation

The direction of sunrise is called Higasi, and three directions of sunset are given: Hinili, Hinata, Hiuke. The eight directions are Higasi, Tami, Hinata, Hisa, Hinili, Hiye, Hiuke, Futo.

Our ancestors' reckoning of time was therefore very close to our own. Yet the life spans attributed to the people of those times

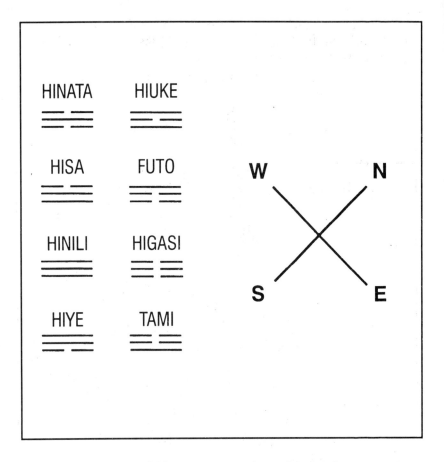

are absolutely incredible. One Sumela Mikoto achieves a given task in 11,005,000,000 years.

That is one reason why today's society cannot accept these ancient chronicles as true. At the end of the Amatu Kami and the beginning of the Kami Yo eras, these ages of billions of years are common. Toward the end of the Kami Yo era, a life-span of several million years becomes the norm. At the beginning of the Fuki Aizu era, this drops to mere tens of thousands, and to a bare few thousands in the middle of the era. At the end of Fuki Aizu Tyo, a human life still averages several hundred years, but at the opening of our own era, it is hardly longer than the life of modern people.

We can imagine that our ancestors lived longer than we do, we can even accept a life span of a few hundred years if we take into account the fact that conditions on earth were different in those days, and that foods that prolonged life were in use. But this can-

not possibly explain life spans of thousands, millions and billions of years.

The notion of counting the years of the physical age is recent and belongs entirely to the second, material civilization. The god-men embodied the life will of the universe, and if they referred to their "age", they were speaking of the age of life itself.

If it is said that they performed a given task in several billion years, that means that the current of Amatu Hitugi took billions of years to achieve this effect.

Later, when life spans begin to shorten, the reference is probably to the beginning of a spiritual descent. Individual age still has no meaning. Later again, it becomes a question of physical descent: what is reckoned is the age of one's blood line. It is only in our era that we begin to count the age of our physical body.

The Takeuti documents are very precise. They state, for example, that in the year 15,000,000,000 of his reign, in Konome halu (Spring), in the month of Kesali tuki (February), Mado hito hi (11th), Sumela Mikoto left on a journey. The name and generation of Sumela Mikoto is given, with his destinations and what he intends to achieve there. Every aspect of civilization — politics, commerce, all types of exchange — are mentioned. The records are too complex, too complete to admit the possibility of forgery. The person fabricating such an enormous amount of information would be literally creating an entire world.

Modern historians are wrong to dismiss these documents so lightly. Along with the written documents, there are also objects and relics of many types. Those who approach the study of these documents honestly and with an open mind will quickly recognize their authenticity. As for students of the Kototama Principle, they should study them carefully, as a way of feeling and understanding humanity's past.

The Buddhist tradition says that we live in a dream society in which everything is upside down in relation to the truth. Reality is hidden, illusion is all we see. There is no point in feeling anger or sadness for the lies and the suffering of our civilization. The material civilization was decreed by our ancestors — by the current of life itself. It must go on to its logical end. Once humanity reaches the limit of this viewpoint, once it can stand no more, the current of society will naturally reverse itself and return to the truth. Then, humanity can leave behind it the karma of the last ten thousand years, as a butterfly emerges from its cocoon.

This is how humanity is guided, this is how civilizations develop. It is the manifestation of Amatu Hitugi, the current of the universal life will.

Amatu Hitugi is what our ancestors have called god in the books they have left us. It is what is inside us — our own life will.

Records

First generation of the Kami Yo era, (21 sub-generations):

The following inventions, practices and achievements are given as being the result of Sumela Mikoto's influence on the development of civilization:

1)   the definition of fourteen kinds of grain food

2) the method of cooking food with fire
3) the creation of utensils and vessels for cooking and eating
4) the basic precepts of medicine
5) the protection of agriculture from insects; the protection of humans from spirits
6) the practice of fishing
7) the art of making clothing
8) the creation of money
9) the creation of writing ink
10) the creation of paper
11) the creation of pens
12) the domestication of cows and horses
13) the practice of cultivating soil before planting
14) the building of houses
15) the preparation of miso
16) the production of salt
17) the creation of mirrors
18) the creation of the lance and the sword
19) the creation of ships of heaven (aeroplanes or spaceships)
20) the creation of water ships
21) the establishment of laws of business, exchange, commerce
22) the building of shrines and the practice of praying
23) the perfection of the Kototama fifty sounds
24) the creation of symbolic letters
25) the creation of maps of the earth

In this same generation, these are the places some of the Sumela Mikoto were buried. Phonetically, these names are very familiar:

7th sub-generation:
    Aziti Kamuti Kuliyu,
    Tiyefu mountain

8th sub-generation:
    Tendjiku Kuni (India),
    Yebelesu sen shrine

11th sub-generation:
    Hiuke Ebilos (North America),
    Siyelanebu, Hoitoni mountains, Monteli

Kami Yo First Generation

Sumela Mikoto of this generation made this Kata Kana of symbols of God-Man and God-Star-Man 51 letters

Kami Yo First Generation

In Kesali Tuki, 300,000 years after taking office, Sumela Mikoto created these letters

WN	LA	MA	NA	SA	A

WA	YA	HA	TA	KA

12th sub-generation:
Hinata Ebilos (South America),
Kolombia, Bogoda

13th sub-generation:
Osutolalia,
Alupu mountain

17th sub-generation:
Osutolalia,
Kesusosi

18th sub-generation:
Yomotu Kuni
Yoloba Temausodo sen

Second generation of Kami Yo era (33 sub-generations):

In the year 686,608,621 of his reign, Sumela Mikoto gave birth to sixteen princes and princess of the five races and sent them out throughout the world. The lands in which they settled took the names of these princes and princesses. These are their lines of descent:

1 Origin of the Chinese nation:

King Banidana Otosuga and his queen Banidana Himi

Banna, King
Idana Kai

Idana Kai Toko

Honkin

Santoko
Fukemme
Susenhe
Nankin
Sansaikin

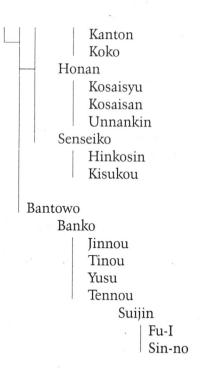

```
        ┐ ┐  │ Kanton
        └─┤  │ Koko
          │ Honan
          │    │ Kosaisyu
          │    │ Kosaisan
          │    │ Unnankin
          │ Senseiko
          │    │ Hinkosin
          │    │ Kisukou
          │
          │ Bantowo
          │   Banko
          │      │ Jinnou
          │      │ Tinou
          │      │ Yusu
          │      │ Tennou
                     Suijin
                        │ Fu-I
                        │ Sin-no
```

2 Origin of the Indian nation:

Ida Kuni Indo Tenjiku Mansan, Black Race King

Tenjiku Nisi Kason (known as Kason, a great saint)
   Tenjiku Majiku Kason

       Tenjiku Ma Kason
         │ Minami Tenjiku Man Sonja
         │ (known as Sonja, a saint)
         │   Nisi Tenjiku Nan Sonja
         │
         │ Higasi Tenjiku Ki Sonja
             Kita Tenjiku Nyo Sonja
             Tiyu Tenjiku Ka Sonja
               │ Indomasitalel Sonja
               │ Halumas Ou Sonja
               │ Kalalaye Sonja
               │
               (far descendant)
               Syaku Son
               (founder of Buddhism)

3 Indotyuulania, Black race king

> Haulaimutai, black race saint
> > Taibi
>
> Atamu Imuin, king
> > Kuinsulando
>
> Abeluhaulame, king
> > Kuinsu
> > Kunburiji

4 Yoiloba Adamu Ibuhi, foundress of the red race

> Afuga Kabu
> Adamu Ibu, king
> Helusya Keluman

5 Sutolalini Hininin Yuitamu, red race founder

> Kuinsuntoani, red race king
> Osutolalia Torens

6 Osutolio Sealando, red race king

> Bainta Salif, king
> > Hineli Ousotolalia, king
>
> Tonkinhi, king
> > Hiuke Ousutolalia, king

7 Asia Syamu Banyuli Musu, founder of the white race

> Alikayui Konka Namu, king
> > Kola To Mamusu, king

Syamu Bankoku Syamu, king
Malatuka, white race king

Fubonsu, king

8 Asia/Annamuno Hanoi, king of the blue race

Tonkinnamu, king
Kambojya, king

9 Afuli Ezifuto, red race king

Nuhia
Suudan Kinea

10 Yohanesu Buluku, king of the blue race

Tulansu Baialu
Natalu
Kilimane

11 Hinata Ebilosu Isomu, founder of the red race

Bulazilu Bala, king
Aluhen Tina Tile

12 Hinata Ebilosu Hialu Hena, founder of the yellow race

Ebilosu Bulaziluko, king
Tamialainusi, king
Ebilosu Mekihiluko, king
Tamia, queen

13 Hiuke Ebilos Hilokone, founder of the yellow race

> Ebilosu Kala Abela, king
> > Miyoi Meo, queen
> Filadelufia, king
> > Miyoi O, king

14 Hiuke Ebilosu Boston, king of the red race

> Yedo Yui Yoi Kulu, king
> Sanfulanisuco Sandosan, king

15 Hiuke Ebilosu Kasukemuko, king of the red race

> Takoamaumi, king
> Esukimalukasu, king
> Hoibo Oito, king
> > Mesiamitoson
> Liton Bulitisi, king

16 Afuli Abisi Amusu, king of the red race

> Konakuli, king
> Fulitaun, king
> Ejifuto Kai, king
> Suezu Akaba, king

These areas of the world received the names of the princes and princesses of the second generation of the Kami Yo era. The major geographical areas are called:

1) Amenoita(under heaven)
   Ilohitoasii Mikoto Kuni   Asia
2) Amenoita Yomotu Mikoto Kuni   Europe
3) Amenoita Afulica Mikoto Kuni   Africa
4) Amenoita Kulohito Oseania Mikoto Kuni   Australia

Kami Yo Second Generation

Tukuri Moji

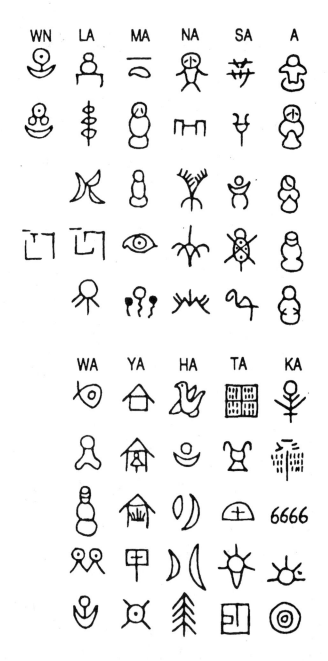

Kami Yo Second Generation

Tori Asi Moji
Bird Leg Letters

5) Amenoita Hinata Ameibilos Mikoto Kuni   South America
6) Amenoita Hiuke Ameibilos Mikoto Kuni   North America

During the second generation of the Kami Yo era, standards of measurement (weight, measures, distances) were established.

These are the burial sites of some of the god men of the second generation of the Kami Yo era:

8th sub-generation	Yomotu Kuni, Monbulan mountain
9th sub-generation	Hinata Ebilosu, Akonkagua mountain
11th sub-generation	Tenjiku Kuni, Yeusuto mountain
14th sub-generation	Hinata Ebilosu, Andesu mountain, Labas
15th sub-generation	Osutolali Kuni, Helufu mountain shrine, Melubolun
16th sub-generation	Hiuke Ebilosu, Atsukinle mountain shrine
17th sub-generation	Hiuke Ebilosu, Loki mountain shrine
22nd sub-generation	Tenjiku Himalaya, Kadomantu shrine
23rd sub-generation	Bolune Kuni, Kinibalu, mountain shrine
24th sub-generation	Papua Kuni, Olania, mountain shrine
28th sub-generation	Itali Kuni, Bolonia
30th sub-generation	Tamialai Kuni (Atlantis), Amelahi mountain shrine
31st sub-generation	Miyoi Kuni (Mu), Hiwawasi mountain shrine
32nd sub-generation	Tamialai Kuni, Amelahi mountain shrine

Third generation of the Kami Yo era, 24th sub-generation:

The documents give many accounts of Sumela Mikoto's travels throughout the world.

Kagulamai, the origins of the Noh dance movements are created. Rituals of prayer are established; Hihilokane wind chimes are made of a metal similar to white gold.

In the year 16,000,000,000 of the reign of Sumela Mikoto, the earth becomes like a molten sea and all life perishes. Sumela Mikoto, with 397 families, boards the floating ship of heaven in Sayoli Sinano Hinotamano Kuni and Akitune Oodaihala Mine. They journey to Amahitamano Kuni (the country of the sun). 5,000,501,000 years later they return, landing on March 1st in Amakosine Nakatso Kuni and begin the reconstruction of all the nations on earth.

Tombs of the Sumela Mikoto of this generation:

10th sub-generation	Hiuke Ebilosu, Logan mountain
11th sub-generation	Yomotu Kuni, Afulika, Kilimastuyalo mountain
12th sub-generation	Hiuke Ebilosu, Popokan Hetolu mountain
19th sub-generation	Hiuke Ebilosu, Kolombia plateau

Fourth generation of the Kami Yo era, 22nd sub-generation:

Civilization was much advanced in this epoch; the practice of medicine and of the different crafts progressed.

Sixth generation of the Kami Yo era, 22nd sub-generation:

Sumela Mikoto boarded the floating ship of heaven, arriving at Tenjiku Kuni Tei Silu. Kalalae, black race king of this land and a great saint, came to greet Sumela Mikoto and to pay his respects.

In the year 1,030,000,000 of his office, on May 10th, Sumela Mikoto arrived at Hilefule mountain in Yomotu Kuni. Adamuibuhi, king of the red race, Kolatomamusu, king of the white race, Kambotya, king of the blue race and others came to pay their respects.

Kami Yo Fourth Generation
Ahiru Moji

LA	HA	SA	A
]ㅏ	Aㅏ	∧ㅏ	Uㅏ
]l	Al	∧l	Il
]T	AT	∧T	OT
]ㅓ	Aㅓ	∧ㅓ	Iㅓ
]⊥	A⊥	∧⊥	U⊥

WA	MA	TA	A
Oㅏ	ロㅏ	[ㅏ	Uㅏ
Ol	ロl	[l	Ul
OT	ロT	[T	UT
Oㅓ	ロㅓ	[ㅓ	Uㅓ
O⊥	ロ⊥	[⊥	U⊥

	YA	NA	KA
Ul	Iㅏ	Lㅏ	ㄱㅏ
	Il	Ll	ㄱl
	IT	LT	ㄱT
	Iㅓ	Lㅓ	ㄱㅓ
	I⊥	L⊥	ㄱ⊥

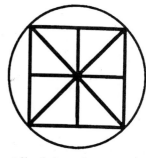

All of the Ahiru Moji
came from this symbol

87

Kami Yo Eighth Generation
Ahiru Kusa Moji

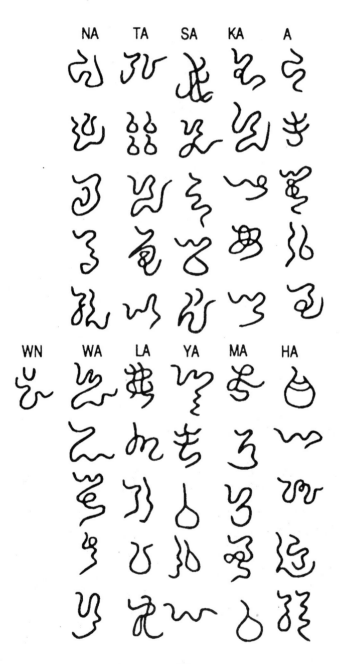

Kami Yo Ninth Generation

Yaso Yorotu Moji

Taught to Miyoi and
Tami Alai countries

Kami Yo Eleventh Generation

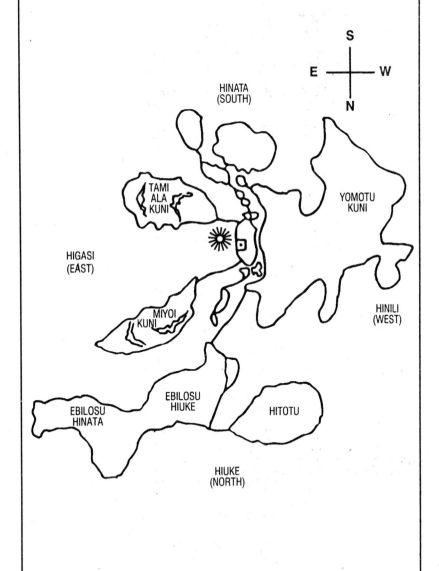

HINATA
(SOUTH)

S

E —— W

N

TAMI
ALA
KUNI

YOMOTU
KUNI

HIGASI
(EAST)

HINILI
(WEST)

MIYOI
KUNI

EBILOSU
HIUKE

HITOTU

EBILOSU
HINATA

HIUKE
(NORTH)

Kami Yo Twentieth Generation

Kami Yo
Twenty-Second Generation
Sakarihimi Moji

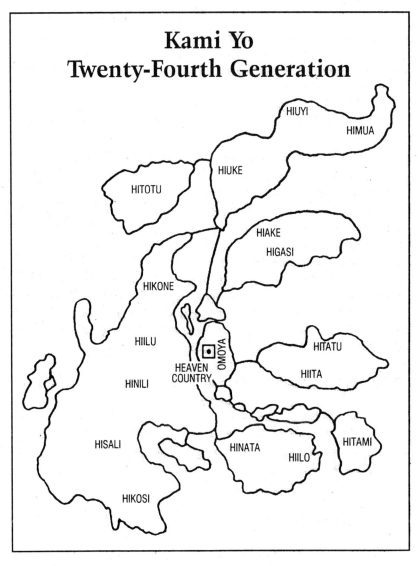

Kami Yo
Twenty-Fourth Generation

In the year 1,180,000,000 of his office, on September 17th, a king arrived in Hinomoto Kuni to pay his respects to Sumela Mikoto, and received the title of king of Ebilosu Kuni.
First generation of the Fuki Aizu Tyo:

The "chrysanthemum" seal was created, with its sixteen petals pointing in the sixteen directions to commemorate the departure of the sixteen princes and princesses of the second generation of the Kami Yo era.

The Hinomalu flag, with a red sun in the center, was created. This is still the flag of modern Japan.

The Gositi no Kili seal, two maple leaves with a maple flower in the center, was also adopted in this epoch. It is still the seal of the Japanese Imperial family.

In the year 1,779,626, on September 10th, Tenno arrived from Edana Kuni (China) to pay his respects to Sumela Mikoto. He received the title of king of China.

In the year 1,797,626, on December 16th, Tinou arrived from Edana Kuni (China) to pay his respects to Sumela Mikoto. He received the title of king of China.

In the year 1,805,626, on February 26th, Jinnou arrived from Edana Kuni (China) to pay his respects to Sumela Mikoto. He received the title of provincial king.

In the year 2,550,000 of his office, on March 15th, Sumela Mikoto with his court visited Ryukyu (Okinawa), using a total of thirty-two Iwakasu fune (water ships), Amenouki fune (floating ships of the air), and Amazolauki fune (floating ships of heaven). Sumela Mikoto possessed a miraculous power enabling him to travel several manli (40,000 kilometers) per day.

Third generation of Fuki Aizu Tyo:

The world's culture was much developed during this epoch. Rituals and ceremonies were established, festival days were decreed and these customs taught all over the world.

The following method was prescribed to ensure a long life:

Daily quantities of food:	
Walawa	1 go
(from birth to 7 years of age)	(143 grams)
Unai (8 to 13)	2 go
Ikasi (14 to 20)	3 go
Hayali (21 to 30)	4 go
Masula (31 to 60)	5 go
Suke (61 to 80)	4 go
Masuke (81 to 100)	3 go
Tinu (101 to 120)	3 go
Matinu (121 to 150)	3 go
Sakio (151 to 380 and over)	3 go

Fuki Aizu Tyo Sixth Generation

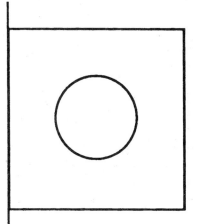

Hino Kami No Maru
Circle of the Sun God

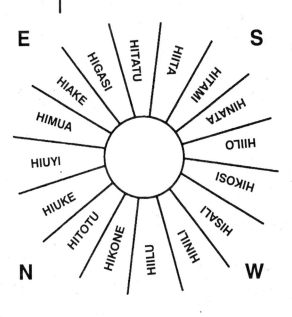

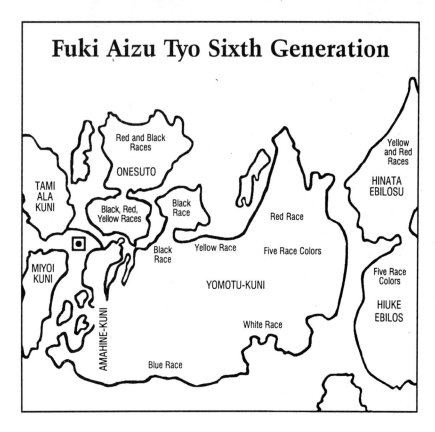

Fuki Aizu Tyo Sixth Generation

Red and Black Races

ONESUTO

TAMI ALA KUNI

Black, Red, Yellow Races

Black Race

Black Race

Yellow Race

Red Race

Five Race Colors

MIYOI KUNI

YOMOTU-KUNI

AMAHINE-KUNI

White Race

Blue Race

Yellow and Red Races

HINATA EBILOSU

Five Race Colors

HIUKE EBILOS

After each meal, Floutyoju Tya, the tea of immortality, should be drunk.

Frequency of sexual relations:

Ikasi (14 to 20)	forbidden
Hayali (21 to 30)	every two days
Masula (31 to 60)	every three days
Suke (61 to 80)	every four days
Masuke (81 to 100)	every six days
Tinu (101 to 120)	every seven days
Matinu (121 and over)	free

Fourth generation of Fuki Aizu Tyo:

In the year 8,345 of his office, on March 2nd, Sumela Mikoto began his travels. He visited Edana (China), Tenjiku (India), Yoiloba, Osutoliosea, Hinata Ebilosu, Hiuke Ebilosu, Afuriejifuto, and enlivened the spirits of kings of the five races.

Fuki Aizu Tyo Tenth Generation

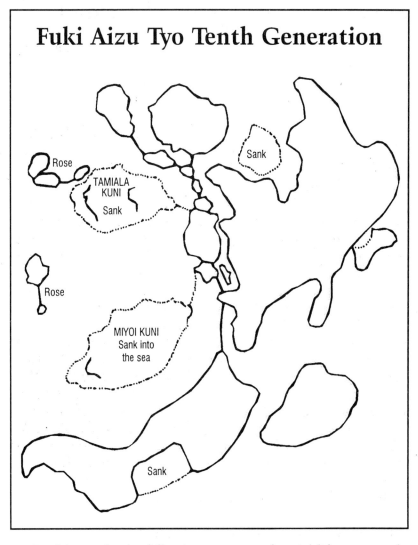

Rose

Sank

TAMIALA
KUNI

Sank

Rose

MIYOI KUNI
Sank into
the sea

Sank

In this epoch, the following patterns of social life were established. These applied to all human beings, male and female:

Walawa	to be well cared for and nourished for strong human growth
Unai	to be taught exercise for physical development
Ikasi and Hayali	to study householding and its attendant arts and skills
Masula	of age to be head of a family
Suke	able to hold an official or governing position

Masuke	able to become the head of a province
Tinu	able to become the head of a country
Matinu (and over)	able to perform service in the entourage of Sumela Mikoto.

Sixteenth generation of Fuki Aizu Tyo:

In the year 85 of his office, on January 20th, Sumela Mikoto gave directives to all the leaders of the world in the correct procedure for the construction of a shrine or temple. He specified that these shrines must be built in high, mountainous regions.

In the year 110 of his office, on June 6th, he began his travels, visiting Edana, Yoiloba, and arriving at a port on the Fransu Balii river. Here, he received the greetings of Lansu, Nansi, Kale, Beluli, Matolii, Lonto, Uyi, Fukalesuto and other kings of the five races, who were accompanied by eight other persons.

Twenty-sixth generation of Fuki Aizu Tyo:

In the year 83 of his office, on February 1st, Sumela Mikoto began his travels, visiting the ports of Asia Aluman, Losia Tuula, Asia Tolu Kuni Koniye, and others. During this journey, 111 of the 317 people who accompanied him were ordered to settle in different lands and made the leaders of their peoples. Twenty-one princes and twenty-three princesses of Sumela Mikoto's family founded new dynasties in these new countries. They were no longer considered Sumela Mikoto's descendants but the founders of new lines.

Sumela Mikoto died at the age of 511.

Thirty-second generation of Fuki Aizu Tyo:

In the year 81 of his office, on May 2nd, Sumela Mikoto began his travels, accompanied by two of his ministers and 327 princes and princesses of his government. They visited Yoiloba Kuni, Asitoluko, and landed at the port of Fulutusa, where kings of the five races came to greet them. They also visited Lomania, Oisutoli, Seluu, Toitu, Suusu, Fulasu, Isubani, Igili, Losii, Uuye, Belusi, Afuga, Alabihailu, Afulinubia, Congo, Ginea, Tenjiku Nagubulu, Edana Daili, Kalusi and other places. 1,300 kings, queens and princes came to pay their respects in these various lands.

Fuki Aizu Tyo Eleventh Generation
Maga Kiri Moji

WN	LA	MA	NA	SA	A
옹	水	몽	ㅋㅏ	자	승
잉	凶	作	기	수	식
루	叩	수	广	帯	舒
西	啩	刁	创	舒	
王	모	고	ㄴ	회	

WA	YA	HA	TA	KA
斜	다	封	자	가
식	추	회	지	기
冊	수	수	즈	키
셍	쉬	최	子	수
竹	쇼	소	王	쇼

Sumela Mikoto died at the age of 491.

Thirty-fourth generation of Fuki Aizu Tyo:

In the year 200 of his office, on November 2nd, Sumela Mikoto returned from Hinata Ebilosu Alubenti Santyago to Hinomoto Kuni in the floating ship of heaven. He gave orders to the guardian family of the Koso Kotai Jingu to hide all of the treasures and documents in their care (over seventy articles), as well as all their methods of education.

Sumela Mikoto died at the age of 503.

Fifty-seventh generation of Fuki Aizu Tyo:

In the month of April of the year 21, there was a great cataclysm in which most of the people of the five races perished.

In the year 187, on October 28th, Sumela Mikoto on his travels passed through Yolotuha Kuni, Lomania Balolatu and arrived at Asia Edana Honten. Fu-I and Sin-no came to Hontenjo to pay their respects.

Fifty-eighth generation of Fuki Aizu Tyo:

Thirty-seven princes and forty-three princesses were sent out to different lands.

The Koso Kotai Jingu was remodeled, and forty-four kings of the five races came to take part in the inauguration of the finished building.

Fu-I and Sin-no arrived from China to study and remained for thirty-six years. They then went back to the Chinese port of Tensin.

Sumela Mikoto died at the age of 491.

Sixty-ninth generation of Fuki Aizu Tyo:

In the year 33, in May, there was great destruction, and once again many people of the five races died. Miyoi (Mu) and Tamialai Kuni (Atlantis) sank into the sea.

Before and in the times following such cataclysms, moti (a type of food), can be seen growing on trees.

In the year 200, on March 26th, Moze (Moses) came to

Fuki Aizu Tyo Twenty-Sixth Generation
Momoki Moji or Yomotu Moji
Peach Tree Branch Letters

WN	LA	MA	NA	SA	A

Hinomoto Kuni and remained for twelve years.

Seventieth generation of Fuki Aizu Tyo:

In the year 107, on October 10th, Syaka (Buddha) arrived from Tenjiku Kuni.

Seventy-first generation of Fuki Aizu Tyo:

In the year 21, in October, there was another catastrophe. It was not very destructive.

In the year 41, on December 22nd, at 5:00 a.m., three suns rose.

In the year 133, on March 1st, Sumela Mikoto returned from the port of Toliko Dosuto.

Sumela Mikoto died at the age of 303.

Seventy-second generation of Fuki Aizu Tyo:

In the year 36 of his office, Sumela Mikoto died at the age of 117.

Seventy-third generation of Fuki Aizu Tyo, First generation of Kami Yamato Tyo:

When he was 100 years of age, on April 1st, Sumela Mikoto, as he was praying in the Koso Kotai Jingu, received an inspiration and spoke the words: "Kami Yamato Yiwale Hiko Mikoto". This was the announcement of the opening of a new era, and it was also his own name, as embodiment of the dimension of the judgment of universal life.

Twelve years later, on April 3rd, he decreed the beginning of the Kami Yamato era, and took the name of Jimmu Sumela Mikoto or Jimmu Tenno (Tenno means Emperor).

124 years later, on April 23rd, Lao-Tsu came to study in Hinomoto Kuni. He remained for two years and returned to China on September 23rd.

Several cataclysms had changed the face of the earth since the seventy-first generation of Fuki Aizu Tyo. The land of Hinomoto Kuni was most affected by the upheavals occurring at the time of

Fuki Aizu Tyo Seventy-First Generation

Kami Yo Moji

WN	LA	MA	NA	SA	A
ン	ラ	マ	ナ	サ	ア
ン	ソ	ヒ	チ	シ	イ
	ル	ム	ヌ	ス	オ
	レ	メ	子	セ	イ
	ロ	モ	ノ	ソ	ヲ

WA	YA	HA	TA	KA
ワ	ヤ	ハ	タ	カ
ヰ	レ	セ	チ	キ
ウ	ユ	フ	ツ	ク
ヱ	エ	ヘ	テ	ケ
ヲ	ユ	ホ	ト	コ

the change from the seventy-first to the seventy-second generation. Its culture was almost entirely destroyed and Jimmu began to import elements of Chinese, Korean and other cultures to reconstruct his country.

From this time on, Sumela Mikoto's travels outside of Japan ceased entirely, and the current of the world's civilization was reversed.

Third generation of Kami Yamato Tyo:

In the year 18, on April 24th, Confucius arrived. He returned to China on March 4th of the year 23.

Sixth generation of Kami Yamato Tyo:

In the year 41, in the month of March, Mao-tu arrived. He returned to China on September 25th of the year 46.

Seventh generation of Kami Yamato Tyo:

In the year 46, on October 10th, Sumela Mikoto gave the title of kings of China to the Sin, a new dynasty. But the Sin did not think this sufficient, and changed the name to Sin Sikote, meaning the First Emperor.

The Chinese kings had received their titles from Sumela Mikoto for 113 generations, since the time of Banko. Sin Sikote ended this tradition.

In the year 72, Jofuku, his minister, arrived with many other officials, saying he wished to study the tradition of permanent-life medicine. His real purpose was to investigate other areas of Japanese tradition like the shrines and the documents of the past. The Japanese government, afraid of Sin's power, received him very courteously.

Sin Sikote, who wished to erase all traces of the past relationship of fealty between China and Japan, had already burned all the ancient records in his country. Jofuku's real objective was to destroy the equivalent records in Japan. But the Japanese had already hidden their ancient chronicles.

From this time on, China began to exist as a completely independent country; Sin Sikote proclaimed Japan to be his colony.

Kami Yamato Tyo Seventh Generation
Hinomoto Katakana
Isohi Moji

NA	TA	SA	KA	A
奈	太	左	加	安

WA	LA	YA	MA	HA
和	良	也	未	波

WN

Eighth generation of Kami Yamato Tyo:

From the first generation of this era, Japanese culture was supplemented by material from other civilizations. The influence of the I Ching, the philosophies of Lao Tsu and Confucius, and Buddhist principles began to re-enter Japan. The traditional Japanese principles and documents proving Japan's ancient status as the world center were endangered.

Sin Sikote's attitude was particularly menacing, and Japan had no armed forces in those days. The use of violence was contrary to its spirit.

In that difficult time, Sumela Mikoto received an order or an inspiration: all the treasures, relics and documents belonging to the Koso Kotai Jingu must be completely hidden. No foreigner must be allowed to see them. Sumela Mikoto then ordered this second hiding.

Ninth generation of Kami Yamato Tyo:

Until this time, all the Japanese shrines were golden in color. Tyo-You, the representative of Bu-Tei (the new Chinese Emperor) came to Japan and instructed Ootutuma Oomimi no Mikoto, (the official in charge of the creation of the nation's shrines), to use natural wood. Returning to China, Tyo-You spread the custom of building golden altars, on the traditional Japanese model. The Chinese have, ever since, built golden shrines.

Eleventh and twelfth generations of Kami Yamato Tyo:

Jesus Christ arrived in Japan. It appears that he came and left several times. Jesus died in Japan at the age of 118.

Thirty-fifth generation of Kami Yamato Tyo:

Mahomet arrived in Japan from Alabia Kuni Meka Siria. He was twenty-four years of age.

Postscript

These are only a few excerpts, roughly summarized. It is clear that until the seventy-first generation of Fuki Aizu Tyo, Sumela

Mikoto traveled all over the world as he and his emissaries taught letters, languages and the basic elements of civilization. The seventy-second Sumela Mikoto of that era had a very short and inactive term of office, and with the seventy-third, who decreed the opening of the new epoch (Kami Yamato Tyo, our modern era), all external traveling, all exertion of influence in foreign lands ceased.

As a complete reversal, culture was no longer exported but brought in from China, Korea, and India. The true principle of Kototama was already hidden.

The world lost Sumela Mikoto's guidance; he became a figurehead, a symbolic god-man who was only the political leader of the country of Japan, a ruler like any other.

It appears that the work of hiding the Kototama principle and the ancient documents was completed by the eighth generation of Kami Yamato Tyo. Japan became a cultural colony of the great nations of the time, China and India. The Chinese characters came to be used for writing the Japanese language; the first book written in this way, the Kojiki, is today believed to be the first book of Japanese culture.

It is generally believed today (and taught in Japanese schools) that no method of writing had been developed in Japan before the adoption of the Chinese Kanji. Many documents exist, however, written in the traditional Kami Yo moji.

These documents are coming to light, and through the efforts of sincere students, the true history of the world will be revealed in the near future.

During the second world war, all the ancient Shinto guardian shrines (but not the new Shinto religious temples) were seized by the government. The Shinto religion supported the militaristic ideology of those days, but the ancient Shinto shrines did not, and suffered for their resistance. Most of the ancient Shinto leaders were put in jail, and Colonel Yano, a Naval officer who had done a great deal of research into the Takeuti documents, was executed.

Over three thousand relics and documents were taken as court evidence. No sanctions were taken in the end, but the documents were never returned. They remained in Tokyo, where fire bombs destroyed them at the end of the war. This was an immeasurable loss for the modern understanding of humanity's past.

My reading of the Bible is that Jehovah was the sixty-ninth Sumela Mikoto of Fuki Aizu Tyo. He gave Moses the order to lead the twelve Hebrew tribes, the Chosen People, who would guide the rest of humanity into the second, material civilization. This can be dated between 3,700 and 3,800 years ago.

The Old Testament is a history of the Hebrew nation in particular, not a history of the world. But if the records of all the world's religious or philosophical traditions are studied, it becomes obvious that they are derived from a single source. The ancient Takeuti documents record the arrival of all the founders of these religions or philosophies as they came to study and practice in the world center. They received their titles from Sumela Mikoto and returned to their own lands to guide their own peoples.

It is time to open our eyes and see this clearly. We are entrenched in the cultural prejudices long habit has bred in us, and it is difficult for modern people to accept this idea. But for billions of years in our past, through the Amatu Kami, Kami Yo and Fuki Aizu eras, the single nation of the world was guided by the world center in Hinomoto Kuni. Sumela Mikoto guided the entire world, and human society was structured according to the principle of the Word.

If human society is issued from a single source, there is no cause for fighting among ourselves. The entire history of our civilization has been one of separation, of raising walls and creating differences. Each group has entered into competition with the others. This has created the situation of the world as we see it today.

Recognizing that this is not right, we must now return to the natural order of human life; to the structure of ancient times. This is a difficult endeavor. All our habits of mind pull us in the opposite direction. To recreate this way of life, each one of us must raise his consciousness from the material viewpoint, which recognizes the world strictly through the experience of the physical senses. We must stand in the highest human dimensions. To reach an understanding of these dimensions, and to find the right path, we must study the Kototama Principle, and also the records of our real past like the Takeuti documents. Other chronicles of this type will probably be discovered in the days to come.

The ancient Sumela Mikoto were perfected human beings. They spoke and acted in direct synchronization with the rhythms of universal life. They were the leaders of society, and formed a universal government, the government of the Messiah. This structure of government is completely different from any form existing today.

The Chosen nation is completing its mission — the perfection of the material and scientific civilization. At the end of this civilization, these people must once again return to the original principle of life: the principle of Kototama, which is the principle of the human life will.

I would like to make a few more comments about the Takeuti documents before going back to their relationship with the Bible.

As I have already explained, the life spans attributed to the Sumela Mikoto of the Amatu Kami and Kami Yo eras are not credible as ages of a posteriori physical life. The god-men of these eras stood on the viewpoint of their **IE** dimension, and thought in terms of a priori time.

Our present body has lived for a certain number of years, but we received that body from our parents, who in turn received their body from their parents. This transmission through the generations goes back to the origin of life. With this physical inheritance, we also carry the hopes, the unfinished work, the mission of our ancestors.

When the ancient god-men spoke in terms of billions of years, they were grasping, through their inspiration, the fact that humanity was as old as the earth, as old as the sun. The current embodied by Sumela Mikoto, the specific wave of cause and effect to which he was dedicated took billions of years — and is still effective today. The share of the mission performed by each individual is not taken into account within this viewpoint.

In those days, nobody would have asked, "How old are you?" in reference to individual physical age. That question belongs to the viewpoint of the materialistic era. Their ancient sense of the passing of a posteriori time was the same as ours: you have just read in the above translations that their year was divided into 12 months of 30 days.

It would seem that the way in which our far ancestors looked at their life was different from ours. We cannot make a distinction between our bodies and our selves. Yet, this body is my house, what I am is the spirit giving life to that house. Our ancestors knew that "I am" lay elsewhere than in the mere physical manifestation. They felt no separation between their self and the universe — they were the universe. The division of time into years, months and days only applies to a posteriori questions.

Much later, in the Fuki Aizu era, this begins to change. Until the fifth generation, the "age" of Sumela Mikoto still ran into tens of thousands of years. The fifth Sumela Mikoto received an order from the ancestors' god-spirits — that is to say from his own human seed: "The life of the people of the five races (i.e. all humanity) cannot go beyond 11,000 years.

It is recorded that Sumela Mikoto wept. He was 11,171 years old when he died, on the 15th of September. The sixth Sumela Mikoto of that era died at the age of 1,638 years, on the 14th of July.

From the 10th generation on, Sumela Mikoto lived less than a thousand years. By the 30th generation, his life span had dropped to a mere 500 years.

There were 73 generations in Fuki Aizu Tyo. We have already seen how the 73rd Sumela Mikoto, upon a revelation received as he was praying, decreed the opening of a new era. He changed his name to Jimmu and became the first Emperor of the present era: Kami Yamato Tyo. He is the founder of the dynasty of Japanese Emperors which has continued unbroken to this day. From the time of Jimmu, the Takeuti documents are only rough notes — but the historical records of our civilization have begun.

The former guides of the world had become the political rulers of single nations. Hinomoto Kuni begins to be called Yamato, and then Nihon (or Japan). To hide more effectively all traces of the civilization of the god-men, Jimmu gave orders to begin importing foreign culture and customs into the country. These outside influences were mainly Chinese (as is shown by the adoption of Chinese Kanji characters) but also Indian, principally through Buddhism.

In this era, the human life span had become much shorter, and with the opening of the material era, we can at last believe that "age" refers to the length of physical existence. The god-men of the Amatu Kami and Kami Yo eras probably counted their time from the first manifestation of the a priori life will. At the beginning of Fuki Aizu Tyo, ages of tens of thousands of years probably refer to a spiritual line of descent — perhaps their line of transmission of the Kototama Principle. Later, "lives" only reach a thousand years or less. This may refer to blood descent, reaching as far back as it could be traced. I am certain that the understanding of the term "age" was completely different in the early eras of the first civilization.

According to the Takeuti documents, it appears that our ancestors began counting their age in terms of physical generations about 2,500 years ago, after the "Jimmu revolution". This notion was imported with other elements of Chinese culture. Even then, the life spans recorded are much longer than ours. But as we have said before, an entirely different mode of life, different food and medicine, and an environment that was not yet polluted can have made a great difference.

In the records of the Amatu Kami era, the creation of the universe and of the finite world are explained. In Kami Yo, the second era, there are 25 generations of Sumela Mikoto — but each is divided into a certain number of sub-generations. All the sub-generations are called "Sumela Mikoto", they all have the same name, but they are different people: the names of their wives and the locations of their tombs are different. This may mean that Sumela Mikoto educated a certain number of disciples, who took that name and spread that influence, and that this was regarded as a "generation". Once again, it must be remembered that physical generation is not the reference, and that the term as it is used here may have spanned many physical generations.

The fact that these different generations of Sumela Mikoto are said to be buried all over the world confirms the existence of lesser centers or "branches" in the care of different god-men.

The first Sumela Mikoto of the Kami Yo era is recorded to have "fathered" 66 princes and princesses, each of which became a teacher of some aspect of civilization. They were sent out as emissaries or appointed kings of different regions.

These princes and princesses were not necessarily blood descendants of Sumela Mikoto. It is much more likely that they were his spiritual children — perhaps directly educated by him, perhaps heirs of his legacy in a more distant sense.

For the most part, the Takeuti documents record the events of Hinomoto Kuni, and the achievements of those who remained there. The journeys made by Sumela Mikoto are detailed, but there is no continuous history of the scattered outposts of the principle. A few documents, for example alphabets created in those outposts, found their way back to Hinomoto Kuni. The documents do not make much distinction however, between what was created in the world center and what was created elsewhere. The only complete record of the foreign lands is the list of the places of death of each of the god-men.

The different generations and sub-generations of the eras of the first civilization are detailed in the translated extracts of the Takeuti documents, earlier in this chapter. I will summarize them rapidly once again:

In the first era, called Amatu Kami, there were seven generations of Sumela Mikoto, the seventh being divided into two sub-generations.

In the Kami Yo era, there were 25 generations of Sumela Mikoto, each being divided into a certain number of sub-generations, each of which bore the same name as Sumela Mikoto.

The Fuki Aizu Tyo, or more exactly the Take Ugaya Fuki Aizu Tyo had 73 generations, the last of which became the first of Kami Yamato Tyo. This era is now in its 126th generation.

In the Fuki Aizu era, Hinomoto Kuni progressively came under Chinese influence. It is in this era that the term "Emperor" first appears as a translation of "Sumela Mikoto". Other lands had kings, Sumela Mikoto was the king of kings. Our meaning of the word "Emperor" is completely different, and only refers to temporal political power.

It is also in that era that it was decided that the name of Sumela Mikoto would only refer to a single person, the world guide residing in Hinomoto Kuni. The Kami Yo era custom of a generation of god-men all bearing the same name is no longer found. The names of individual leaders begin to be recorded. The principle is already being clouded.

I will try to give the clearest possible explanation of the title of Sumela Mikoto.

Those who have grasped the content of each sound as their own life rhythm need no explanation, and it is impossible to explain with the words of our languages. An explanation uses symbols, the truth of the sound can only be found in the sound itself. But I will try to give some idea of this meaning.

Sumela means that the final truth, the complete content of Kototama Futomani is grasped. From this viewpoint, it becomes possible to judge a posteriori human society. *Mikoto* is a person capable of guiding civilization into the proper channel. Sumela Mikoto is the highest capacity of a god-man.

When the god-men began to be referred to by their individual names, it may simply have been a notion of the scribes or translators of the documents, in an effort to create a clear record. I think however that it is an indication of a change, perhaps already a lessening of the capacity of the god-men. The current of Amatu Hitugi had perhaps already begun to turn; the hiding of the Kototama Principle may have already begun.

The missionaries who hid the Kototama Principle

I explained earlier that the task of translating the principle of Kototama Futomani into symbolic, indirect references with the object of hiding it from society had already begun 8,000 years ago when Fu-I and Sin-no came to Hinomoto Kuni. We do not know the number of people who worked to achieve this. From the original decision to hide the principle until about 2,000 years ago, there may have been 144,000. This number is given in the Bible, and may apply to either the missionaries of the first or second civilizations.

I believe the missionaries of the first civilization are the ancestors of the Celts. They went abroad to teach the life principle and to educate all the nations of the world. The Old Testament explains that the missionaries of the second civilization were the twelve tribes of Israel. Of course, the tasks were not so clearly parceled out between Celts and Hebrews, and many Celts may have contributed to the establishment of the second civilization.

Still, this would not have been easy. The emissaries of the first civilization were teaching the Kototama Principle; those of the second were hiding its contents behind symbolic representations. Ordinary people would hardly have trusted a teacher who suddenly began speaking against all his former principles. It would have had to be a slow and subtle process.

More difficult yet: the missionaries of the first civilization were completely dedicated to their task. The more committed they were, the harder the change.

In the ancient records, the word *Seito* is used to refer to a group of god-men. This is probably the origin of both the words "saint" and "Celt". The saints of the second civilization have been the only humans of our times whose capacity approached that of the god-men. The god-men had complete confidence in the Kototama Principle, they knew it was the truth of life. They recognized the necessity of the establishment of the second civilization, but it must have broken their hearts to have to work in this direction.

For the last 3,000 years, the founders of all religions, all philosophies, all mystical or occult aspects of human culture like astrology or numerology, have had as a mission the veiling of the truth. They were all working for the perfection of the second civilization.

The earliest among them were acting consciously, the latter followed in the wake of their teachers without knowing the deeper effect of what they were doing.

With the passing of time, no one doubted any longer that the material way was the path civilization must take. It had become impossible to even conceive of another approach. Humanity merely had to wait a little longer, and science would solve every problem. It was only a question of time.

Today, these doubts are surfacing again. Humanity has stopped trusting science, medicine, and the word of experts. It does not know what to put in their place, but it is sure that something is missing.

At the beginning of our civilization, the missionaries were talking about the truth in symbolic terms. Therefore the original founders knew the principle, and chose to present it in parables. The symbolism used was different according to the language or background of each teacher, but at bottom, they were all referring to the same thing. It is obvious that they had all studied the Kototama Principle.

Mahomet, the founder of Islam, was the last of the foreign missionaries to come to Hinomoto Kuni. His name, like those of the founders of the other religions of the world, is mentioned in the Takeuti documents.

The last generations of god-men of the first civilization knew that the Kototama Principle was the only reality of human life, but they had come to understand that a civilization based on it could not satisfy humans who had no personal grasp of it. They decided to hide the fundamental principle of life behind symbolic explanations and began to guide society in the way it demanded: toward the satisfaction of the physical desires. They knew what a cruel society would result once human capacity turned all of its energies toward the material viewpoint. They knew before they began that there must be countless sacrifices along the way.

They also knew that when the material civilization was perfected, science would be able to see the existence of the truth — from the outside. The scientific viewpoint can never grasp the truth itself or recognize it as its own source. But humans are coming to see the limitations of science. Science has already reached the end of matter and found the void; where else is there for it to go? Now that we have reached this point, it must become clear that we have come to the end of this type of civilization.

Eight thousand years of sacrifice have gone into the development of this society; we have paved the way with the destruction of every thing on the earth. When we realize what we have done, how much we have broken, we may realize how great a crime it was, and how much we have to regret. We may apologize then, crying to the source of our life to be forgiven — but that will not restore what has been destroyed. The end of our civilization will be like this, and that end is coming very soon.

Our political, religious and scientific leaders have no idea how to get us out of the situation we are in. They can only apply solutions derived from the viewpoint which created the difficulty in the first place. Nothing can be done with the knowledge of the second civilization. The ill cannot also be the cure.

The god-men saw all this clearly when they made their decision. About ten thousand years ago, Sumela Mikoto left very clear orders as to what we must do when we reach this time. He left us Amatu Norito, which tells us to abandon, to throw away the viewpoints of philosophy, science and religion. To change the contents of our Amatu Kanagi and Amatu Sugaso knowledge and to return to the original viewpoint of the Amatu Futonolito principle.

There are two types of missionaries for the development of the second civilization. The first uses material power, the power of arms or of money, to prove it is the strongest thing on earth. The essence of this approach is competition, its ideal is security. In the Kanagi viewpoint and education, the strong devour the weak, and the strongest is also the happiest.

The second type represents the policy and education of the spiritual side. It illustrates the **A** dimension Sugaso viewpoint, and demonstrates that happiness and harmony are to be found in the arts, philosophy, or religion.

At the very beginning of the second civilization, the first missionaries chose one or the other of these approaches, knowing very well their real meaning. They were not allowed to talk directly about the Kototama Principle, but they had studied it and they knew the reason for hiding the truth.

In the next chapter, I will explain more fully the contents of the three principles of Kototama. Amatu Kanagi looks from the material viewpoint, Amatu Sugaso from the spiritual viewpoint. The first type of missionaries set up the Amatu Kanagi principle as its god, the second deified Amatu Sugaso. But the two are interchangeable. Both were necessary parts for the development of our civilization. Either side can be used to further the purpose. If we want to make a distinction, it can be said that Moses belonged to the first group of missionaries and Jesus to the second.

Once the Kototama Principle was hidden, every aspect of human culture reflected one or the other of the two basic viewpoints of our civilization. The later generations representing each of them — the great men on one side or the other — knew nothing of the original principle. They simply took the symbolic knowledge in which they had been educated a step further. Our far ancestors created the symbolic representations of the capacities of the life dimension — the later generations took the symbols for reality. If this view of reality seemed a little disjointed or incomplete, it was because, from the religious viewpoint, man could not know God, and from the scientific viewpoint, there was no absolute truth or coherence, no universal law.

In Moses' time, when the symbols were first introduced, it was possible to understand what they referred to. By the time of Jesus or Mahomet, there no longer was any opportunity for the majority of people to study the principle, and no way of understanding the allusions of the first missionaries.

The scholars of the later generations read the books of the first missionaries, and began to interpret their obscurities. They explained them according to their personal references.

The following generation, educated in this interpretation, adds its own interpretation, imagination, and references. Compounded over the centuries, this is the foundation of our entire system of education: the commentaries on commentaries.

This has also been the fate of each "discovery" of our own civilization. After a few generations only, it is impossible to know what was really in the minds of the great men of our time. Each of their students starts his own school.

When books date from a much earlier era, modern scholars believe they are obscure because they were written in a more primitive time, when knowledge was less advanced. They therefore try to interpret them according to the modern vision of the world.

Oriental medicine is based on the book of the *Yellow Emperor*. Modern readers of this book only look at the surface meaning of the words. They take it literally, and either reject it as hopelessly primitive or try to pull its meaning around to fit their own interpretation. No one today can imagine that the Yellow Emperor's book is a symbolic explanation of the final truth of life.

Still, every human being has at his core an inner voice. Our life is still guided by the dimension of the life will. We can sometimes feel a certain sense, an unreasoned reluctance or eagerness to do a certain thing. Today, more and more people are searching for the truth of their existence.

But how do they search for it? They begin reading. What do they read? Religious, philosophical, or medical books. They hope to find themselves in ancient religious texts or in modern scientific books. Their teachers tell them to study sacred books. They read the Bible — and its commentaries. They study theories based on other theories and fall into a deeper confusion.

This approach leads straight back into the current of the materialistic, scientific civilization. It is not the road to the essence of your self.

The founders of our civilization — the first generations of leaders to hide the Kototama Principle — spoke always in symbolic terms. If we base our study on their books, we are searching only in the dimensions of **UO** or **AO** acquired knowledge, on the scientific or spiritual side.

Religious and scientific books can be read and understood in an infinite number of ways. Anyone can make what they like of an individual theory; they will only arrive at a personal understanding, adding another stone to the wall of the prison. The truth is not an individual matter; it is universal or it is not the truth. No two people understand the symbols of our ancestors in the same way. Each person is convinced that his understanding is right.

Even this book, which talks directly of the Kototama Principle, is a symbolic explanation. I am writing in an intellectual language, with letters which we have agreed to accept as representing certain sounds. None of this has anything to do with the inner truth of our life rhythms.

If two students of Kototama compare their understanding of what I am trying to say, it will not be the same. It will never be the same until it is expressed in pure sounds, each grasped and compared with the reality of our life rhythms.

The form of understanding based on acquired knowledge is as limited as our intellectual form of communication. The thinkers of our entire civilization have spent their lives arguing about the meaning of words. The different students of a teacher will have a slightly different understanding; their own students will be at war. The second world war was fought because of the faith their followers had in the individual theories of Hitler and Tojo.

It is possible to take Saint John's "In the beginning was the Word", and interpret it as "The Bible is the Word of God". Neither Christ nor Saint John ever said that, but that is what Christian priests now teach. If they are asked what this means, they will answer: "Everything was created by the Word of God". But if you ask: "What is God?", they don't know. "What is the Word of God?" "The Bible".

There are many good things in Christianity. It is good to love one another and to help the poor. But Christianity, filtered through the symbolic explanations given by Christ himself, then through the written gospels, and then through the understanding of the priests, is not the truth of life.

Each generation is led a little further away from the real hidden meaning of the symbolic structures on which our cultures are based. Each generation brings its changes. Add to that the desire to be right, and you arrive at today's version of the world's religions and philosophies. Each generation believes it is bringing improvements to the original theory. In this civilization, expansion is always an improvement, but what expands too far is torn away from its roots.

With the means of communication technology has provided, we suddenly have access to the legacy of all the founders — to the origins of all the different cultures on earth. It is only natural that we should mix what seems most attractive in each. That is the content of our present knowledge. If the founders of our civilization look upon what it has become, they must smile a bitter smile.

A few people have come to see our present civilization as a swollen, muddy current which must be purified. The only way to do this is to go back to the source. The source of our civilization is also the source of our life — society is our creation. In some places in the world, a few people who have listened to their inner voice are now speaking about this source. But are they speaking about the same thing? Where is the source, what is it? They don't seem to be able to show it clearly. Perhaps I am lacking in courtesy, but I feel that most of them are only referring to the words of the founders of their culture. That is still a symbol, and not the real source.

They are calling their people to return to the purity of the original missionaries' symbols, but they do not know what these missionaries were referring to. Not all of them have even gone back this far, and the greatest among them do not know of the existence of our ancestors' final principle of the human life dimension — the Kototama Principle.

In Japan, until the second world war, tradition had it that whoever attempted to decipher the original meaning of the Kojiki would die. Therefore, it has always been known that the Kojiki had a hidden meaning. The Kojiki is Kototama Futomani, symbolized as a mythology. Its content was a hidden treasure; the re-translation into its original meaning was entirely the responsibility of the Sumela Mikoto of Hinomoto Kuni. No other person could meddle with it. This was an order dating from the time of the decision to hide the principle and it was Sumela Mikoto's absolute order: no one must touch it until the time comes.

According to this prophecy or order, the translation of the Kojiki was begun by Meiji, 123rd Emperor of Kami Yamato Tyo. Even then, the work was begun secretly. It was continued through three generations and completed by Ogasawara Sensei. Before it was published, Hirohito, 125th Emperor of Kami Yamato Tyo had announced that he was a common man and not a god.

When he began the translation, Meiji was still in the position of a god-man. The spiritual descent of Sumela Mikoto was concluded with Hirohito Showa. Our civilization had nearly run its course, the hiding of the principle had served its purpose, and the interdiction was lifted. The last god-man stepped down from his divine position. By that act, he lifted the ban and made the treasure his ancestors had protected for so long accessible to the common people.

I said above that the people who, having opened their inner eye, are today telling their followers to return to the source, do not know the real meaning of the words of their ancestors. I feel they cannot reach the origin of human life because, in the entire world, and even in Japan, almost no one has seriously practiced and grasped the contents of the Kototama Principle. Few people in the world today even know of its existence, and it is a very different thing to know of it and to grasp it as the final truth of life. Modern-day Japanese people know the word "Kototama", but they have no idea of its content.

I say that without the Kototama Principle, it is impossible to understand the words of the founders of our civilization. What they were referring to, in symbolic terms, was Kototama.

Today, humanity is struggling to free itself from its own doubts and fears. People strive for a quiet mind, they want to find the final truth. But that is only the desire of the **A** dimension emotional world. It is like looking for the Bluebird: it is not enough. In the Yamato language, the color blue is Aoi. The bird of **AOI** cannot know its own origin or lead the children back to their own source.

Humanity has already spent many thousands of years wandering in the world of **A** dimension. That is not where the key to our ancestors' words can be found.

We have lost the consciousness of the life dimension, in which there is no separation. All we know are the theories based on individual, personal experiences. We have created artificial languages and allowed our vision of the world to be directed by them — and not by the sound rhythms which are the reality of the thing they name. Every word we speak has been learned from others, and then given a personal sense based on our own experiences. From this individual standpoint, we can only seek individual gratification. This takes the shape of material belongings, power, honorable positions. We have gone to the length of enslaving other nations in the name of material gain. We have completely lost our freedom, we have even lost the meaning of the word "freedom".

This viewpoint reached its logical conclusion when it took its most advanced material techniques, and created the atomic bomb: the destruction of the core of matter itself. That is the absolute evil.

The serpent is biting its own tail. We have created this power, and now we are terrified of it. We have created all the things which are threatening us today. There is no danger in our society which we did not bring into being. The present situation of all human cultures today is the perfect proof that the road we are following is diametrically opposed to the way of life and truth.

We are asking for life, expecting it with all our inner desires — but we cannot see our way to it because we cannot understand the real meaning of the principle our ancestors, in their divine love, left us in a disguised form.

We have built our civilization on the knowledge and experience of the lower dimensions' capacities. It has expanded, and we have called this an improvement. We are proud of our success, it bolsters our personal pride and beliefs. When we study our ancestors' epoch and see, from the outside, how they lived, we laugh at them and call them primitive. It is impossible, on the basis of the fragmented material evidence which remains, to see the great and deep principle on which they based their lives.

We had to follow the material path because we could not understand the life principle. We have suffered a great deal to learn that the material viewpoint is not enough. No human can be happy as long as he is cut off from his own life dimension.

I will now go back to the Takeuti documents, and transcribe some of the excerpts from the historical records which mention Moses, Jesus and Mahomet.

Moze-Lomyo-Las (Romulus)

"The 69th Sumela Mikoto of Fuki Aizu Tyo was Kamu Taru Toyo Suki Kantaru Wake Toyo Suki Sumela Mikoto. In the 200th year of his reign, on March 6th, Moze-Lomyo-Las, political king of the five races, arrived in Hinomoto Kuni from the Sinai mountain in the land of Alabia Akaba. He came to pray in the Koso Kotai Jingu for the ancestors of the five races."

The Koso Kotai Jingu is divided into an inner and an outer shrine. In the outer, one prays for the ancestors of Yomotu Kuni (foreign lands); in the inner, for the ancestors of Hinomoto Kuni.

"While he was there, Moses made the stones of the Ten Commandments. There were three different Jikai, or sets of commandments: Omote Jikai: the front, Ura Jikai, the back, and Shin Jikai, the true commandments."

These would be the Commandments belonging to the Kanagi, Sugaso, and Futonolito principles. Moses' mission was to spread the Omote, or outermost principle.

"He engraved them on veined agate and other semiprecious stones [there were five pieces] and presented them to Sumela Mikoto".

"Moze married Omuro Hime Mikoto, a grand-daughter of the 63rd Sumela Mikoto of Fuki Aizu Tyo. He then remained for twelve years in Hinomoto Kuni, and returned to Sinai mountain."

The dates given mean Moses came to Hinomoto Kuni 694 years before Jimmu decreed the change of era, or 3,344 years ago. The stones engraved by Moses are still kept in the Koso Kotai Jingu.

Omuro Hime later changed her name to Roma Hime Mikoto. Moses went to Italy with his family to create the Roman branch. He remained there until it was well organized, then left it in the care of his son Romulus. When the Takeuti documents record the arrival of "Moze-Lomyo-Las", they may be referring to more than one person. Lomyo-Las could either be a part of Moses' name, or the name of a son who had come with him.

"Moze left Lomyo-Las and Numyo-Bon-Hilyus in Rome and returned to Hinomoto Kuni with Roma Hime on June 25th of the year 421 of the same reign: in the time of the 69th Sumela Mikoto of Fuki Aizu Tyo.

He died on November 25th of that same year, at Hotatu Mountain in the region of Notono."

The above excerpts are quoted from the book of Colonel Ikutaro Yano. Colonel Yano, a naval officer, was a serious student of the ancient documents. When the second world war broke out, he was put in prison for speaking out against the war and the entire policy of the government. He died in his cell, from poison.

In prison, he wrote a series of essays which were smuggled out by friends — as a colonel, his influence probably gave him some latitude of action. These papers were handed on to his wife, who was expressly forbidden to open them until the end of the war.

The official report said that Colonel Yano had died of disease. When his wife came to claim his body, it showed clear evidence of poisoning. After the war, Mrs. Yano published her husband's essays in a book.

Colonel Yano had studied the Takeuti documents before the war, and apparently made copies of some of them. I mentioned earlier that a great many documents were destroyed at the end of the war, burned in Tokyo by incendiary bombs. The documents Colonel Yano refers to no longer exist, but what he says is confirmed by the notes of Ogasawara Sensei, my late teacher. Before the war, Ogasawara Sensei worked for Colonel Yano for a short time as his secretary.

In Ogasawara Sensei's opinion, Colonel Yano was too much inclined to the **A** dimension viewpoint. He immersed himself in the study of the Takeuti documents without having the guideline of the Kototama Principle, and seems to have somewhat lost his sense of reality. Ogasawara Sensei had already begun to study the life principle, and he soon began working for Yamakoshi Sensei. Colonel Yano's book was printed in 1964 under the title "Sin Lu Seitan": "The Real Book of the Divine Spirit".

Another trace of the documents burned during the war remains in the books of Kiku Yamane. This lady was educated in a mission school and became a Christian. Her husband was doing research in the Takeuti documents, and she was shown the references to Christ which they contained. This must have been quite a shock. Jesus Christ in Hinomoto Kuni? She studied the documents and did a great deal of research in the regions of Japan where Christ was reported to have lived and worked.

Mrs. Yamane's work deals principally with the life and achievements of Jesus, but she also quotes the passages relating to Moses. As you can see, the discrepancies are very small:

"Moze-Lomyo-Las arrived in Hinomoto Kuni in the 200th year of the reign of Kamu Taru Toyo Suki Kantaru Wake Toyo Suki Sumela Mikoto, on March 16th. Moze-Lomyo-Las arrived from Yomotu Kuni [foreign lands] and remained for twelve years. In this time he made ten Commandments for the law of the people of the five races of the world. They were engraved on precious stones and presented as a gift to Sumela Mikoto. Sumela Mikoto kept these stones in the Koso Kotai Jingu, his principal shrine. This was 660 years before the Jimmu revolution."

"Moze married princess Omuro Hime and raised seven children. Sumela Mikoto named Moze the guide and protector of Yomotu Kuni."

[Mrs. Yamane does not specify which foreign land; this may have meant that Moses was given the responsibility for the foundation of a foreign center: Rome according to Colonel Yano.]

"Moze died in his 583rd year, and was buried in Nomo canyon in Noto Hotatu Mountain. A part of his tomb and of its contents was later moved to Etyu no Kuni and to the Kuri Ha [Korea] Annebo mountains, to create new shrines."

"Omuro Hime died on February 7th of the 77th year of Sumela Mikoto's reign, at the age of 461, and was buried with Moses on the Noto Hotatu Mountain."

This last date must either be a mistake or a misprint: both Colonel Yano and Mrs. Yamane herself place Moses' arrival in the 200th year of this Sumela Mikoto's office.

Mrs. Yamane also adds some of her personal ideas, and these can be unpleasant. She adds:

"Moses' Ten Commandments, the Omote Jikai, Ura Jikai and Shin Jikai are hidden in Japan. The Freemasons, a secret Jewish organization, are looking for these stones. The Jewish people believe that the nation who holds them can conquer and control the entire world. They believe the stones are being secretly held by occult Jewish leaders."

Actually, Moses' stones are simply kept in the Koso Kotai Jingu among the treasures entrusted to the Takeuti family. Mrs. Yamane interprets their influence in terms of "conquering the world". Nowhere in the ancient documents is there a mention of this word or concept. The fundamental meaning of the Amatu Futonolito Kototama Principle simply does not contain anything approaching the present-day sense of "conquest". There is no place for that notion, it cannot exist in the life principle.

The ancient god-men were completely free of knowledge in the a posteriori sense of the word. They had completely grasped the Kototama Principle and the contents of their own life, and they lived completely in the a priori viewpoint. It is impossible for people of this capacity to use words like conquer, control, steal. They were completely devoid of the sense of competition.

The term used in the ancient documents is Koto Muke Wasu: create complete understanding and harmony through communication — through the spoken word. In other words: explain the fundamental principle of life, show it as a way of civilization, and through this understanding of the source of life, bring all of humanity to a perfect agreement and cooperation. This sense cannot be translated as "to conquer."

If I ask you to open your self to the Kototama Principle and you begin to practice in this way, we will naturally agree. There is no conquest involved. "Whoever holds those stones can control the world?" This is a very serious error. And how disappointing it would be if our ancestors' words, engraved on Moses' stones, should only come to this.

I have explained this to show how the interpretations she gives in her book could have grave consequences. Why and how could the nation holding an inanimate object control the world? She may have meant it in a patriotic sense: Moses' stones are in Japan, and therefore one day Japan will control the world. But a study like hers is not the place for displaying irresponsible personal sentiments of this kind. There are very few published studies of the Takeuti documents and her interpretation must influence all those who come to read it. If the impression she gives is involuntary, she is no longer here to rectify it.

The printed word has a very great weight in our culture, and a single careless word can endure through many generations.

Both Colonel Yano and Mrs. Yamane are dead. They both studied the civilization of our ancestors, but only in its historical aspects, through the Takeuti documents. There are slight discrepancies between their books (dates for example), and their viewpoints are somewhat different. Some of the things they have written are not acceptable to me, but I cannot change or correct the contents of their books. I can only quote them as they are.

Colonel Yano's work seems to be based directly on the original documents, before their destruction in the war. Mrs. Yamane, on the other hand, worked after the destruction of the documents, with translations made by other scholars. The dates and explanations given by Colonel Yano seem more faithful: Mrs. Yamane does not seem as sure, and she adds too many personal comments and interpretations.

I am not a historian, and I am less interested in the ancient chronicles than in searching for the final content of the Kototama Principle. History as such has never attracted me, I have never felt it to be reliable. I am transcribing here the work of historians to illustrate a point, but I am not qualified to say how correct that work is.

The study of the ancient historical records is also very important for the development of our civilization. The work that has been done is very valuable, but it must always be remembered that history, like archaeology, only brings to light external, material evidence. It only shows the surface of events and the physical objects used in daily life. Archaeologists could prove the authenticity of the Takeuti documents, but this would not help anyone understand them.

I feel that the scholarly approach is not complete and cannot reach the essence of the civilization of ancient times. That is why I have not made more efforts in this direction. I only want to grasp the content of the Kototama Principle in myself, as my own source, through my practice. The capacity of my own life can then recognize the real meaning of the words of our ancestors. This is the only way to be certain of their content as the totality of our own inner capacity.

We must then try to stand on the same viewpoint as our ancestors.

Historians cannot reach this kind of certainty. Mrs. Yamane states that the Jewish people believe that the nation who holds the stones of the Ten Commandments controls the world. The Jewish people themselves have never said this as far as I know. Mrs. Yamane gives no reason for the making of the Ten Commandment stones. The number 10 means nothing to her. Moses could as well have engraved eight or twenty Commandments. She cannot look deeper than the surface. For her, Moses could have engraved his Commandments at any time, on any stone, anywhere.

About twenty years ago, I visited a Hopi Indian village in the state of Arizona, and met the elders of the tribe. The chief told me that the Hopi people had Moses' tablets of the Ten Commandments. He also told me one of their traditional stories: "A long time ago, the Great Spirit (their name for a god-man) left the Hopi people and went away over the sea. When he left, he said: 'When the time comes, I will come back to you. But until that day, you, the Hopi, can never choose the leader of your race. You can never select one man to lead you all; when it is necessary to make a decision, you must all discuss it together, and come to an agreement'."

The Hopi nation has always strictly followed that order, and will continue to do so. There is no rank among them, no hierarchy except that of age. When I said I spoke with their chief, I meant the eldest of the elders, the one who was most respected among them.

A few years ago, I heard that this man had passed away. When I met him, his people told me that he was 114 years old. I would have judged him to be about 90. The ten or eleven elders all said they were over 90 but I felt them to be younger. However, there are no records of the dates of their births, so I was happy to accept their way of counting. It is interesting, at any rate, to find the tradition of the Ten Commandments in an American Indian culture.

Both Colonel Yano and Mrs. Yamane write that when Moses-Romulus arrived in Hinomoto Kuni, he already had the title of king of the five races. There is no previous record of him in the Takeuti documents. That means he probably did not receive his title directly from Sumela Mikoto, but from a god-man in Egypt or in Greece. He then accomplished the first part of his mission, which is recorded in the Old Testament, and came to Hinomoto Kuni to report or to be presented to Sumela Mikoto.

The books of both authors put a hyphen between the names Moses and Romulus, but both seem to be referring to a single person. As I said earlier, he either arrived with his son or later gave his own second name to his son.

In both books, Moses is shown arriving single to Hinomoto Kuni and marrying the princess Omuro. They have seven children in twelve years, and the entire family leaves to return to Mount Sinai. The next time he appears in the chronicles, Moses has finished organizing the branch city of Rome and is returning to Hinomoto Kuni with Roma (Omuro Hime), leaving Romulus and Numyo Bon Hilyus in charge.

Seven children in twelve years seem too many for the god-men of that time. Could he have gone to Rome with his eldest children and had the others there? The Takeuti documents say he returned to Mount Sinai, then speak of him in Rome. They do not specify how long he lived there, or how long it took to organize the Roman center.

Moses' work with the people of Israel as recorded in the Old Testament would have taken place before he went to Hinomoto Kuni for the first time. He was already a king when he arrived. He had already worked with angels — or god-men — on a very important mission. He was recognized as the leader of his people. The Old Testament says that he was still a strong man when he went back to Mount Sinai and disappeared:

> "...to this day no one knows his burial place. Moses was 120 years old when he died; his sight had not dimmed nor had his vigor failed." (Deuteronomy 34: 6-7)

It is at this point that he could have gone to Hinomoto Kuni. Moses was only a king when he arrived, and not yet a god-man. He probably became one later, upon his marriage with a princess or god-woman.

When Moses died in Hinomoto Kuni, he was well over 500 years old. He was 120 when he finished his work with the tribes of Israel. This gives him all the time he needed to go to Hinomoto Kuni, spend twelve years there, go back to Mount Sinai and from there to Italy, create and organize Rome and return to Hinomoto Kuni. His children would also have had time to grow up and be ready to carry on his work.

The information given in the Takeuti documents about the life of Moses is startling, but unfortunately a little vague. There are no details of the creation of Rome. All this was happening very far away from Hinomoto Kuni, and there was so much to record the world over!

At any rate, the Takeuti documents, incomplete as they are, exist. Somewhere in the Middle East, or in Rome, there may be much more complete records, written from the local viewpoint. Many new documents may yet come to light. I hope very much that each of the important branches kept records of their surrounding areas.

The Takeuti documents, as I have said before, deal mainly with the events of Hinomoto Kuni, and are often incomplete when it comes to those of other lands. This is no reason to disregard them completely, or to dismiss them as the work of madmen or forgers. It is however not my responsibility to prove or disprove them. They exist, and I quote from them and from the work of those who have studied them.

I believe it was in 1965 that I met in Paris the historian I mentioned earlier, who was also a Freemason. I gave him a short explanation of the Kototama Principle and showed him the Japanese books containing references to Moses' visits to Hinomoto Kuni. He told me that Moses' real name was Imusha, and asked me the meaning of this name in the pure sounds of Kototama.

Written in Chinese characters, *I* is the wild boar, *Musha* the samurai. The wild boar charges straight ahead and is afraid of nothing: that would be the modern interpretation of the spirit of Moses.

It is slightly different in the pure sounds of Kototama. **I** is the life will, manifested as **MU**, the space of physical senses. With this desire of the senses, it creates **SHIA**. **SHI** is the single line, **YA** is the arrow, straight to the mark.

Jesus Christ

One day, after the second world war, the 69th of the Takeuti line (the father of the current head of the family) was re-arranging the shrine's treasures when he came upon a cache of records referring to Christ. For this traditional Shinto practicant, this was a considerable surprise. Mr. Takeuti had disliked both Christians and Christianity, but his attitude changed completely after making this find.

Jesus, in a prophecy, had given the date of his return. These documents were found on that very day.

Mr. Takeuti knew Mrs. Yamane and knew that she was a Christian. He showed these documents to her, and they agreed that they must be published. Since it was better that a Christian be the author of such a work, Mr. Takeuti asked Mrs. Yamane to write a book on the authentic life of Christ.

In the Takeuti documents, his name is given as *Iesu Kirisuto*.

"In the time of Sui-Nin Tenno, the 11th Sumela Mikoto of Kami Yamato Tyo, Kirisuto came to Hinomoto Kuni".

By this time, the name "Nippon" as well as "Emperor" had begun to replace the traditional terms.

"Kirisuto escaped from peril in his own land and landed at Hati no He Harbor, in the region of Tiji no Kuni. He lived in the village of Herai until the age of 118".

The record is much clearer about Christ than about Moses. After a great deal of research in the Takeuti documents and in different regions of Japan, Mrs. Yamane was able to reconstruct the life of Christ. She wrote two different books: "The True History of the World", published in 1964 (from which I took the quotes mentioning Moses), and another, exclusively on Christ, quoted here.

"In the time of Keiko, 12th Emperor of Kami Yamato Tyo, Kirisuto passed away in his 118th year in the village of Herai".

It would seem that Kirisuto achieved a great deal in Japan itself. He worked at the development of the different regions, particularly the north.

Mrs. Yamane made many interesting finds, but they are outside our subject.

According to her book, Jesus arrived in Japan when he was 18, landing at Noto Hotatu Harbor, the place made famous by the tomb of Moses and Omuro Hime.

Christ started studying with the chief priest of the Koso Kotai Jingu. He was his disciple for about five years. The record tells us that he worked hard and learned many different subjects: letters, ceremonials and prayer, history, astronomy...and of course the basic principle of ancient Shinto: the Kototama Principle.

At the end of his five years of study, Jesus received the title of king of the red race and was sent back to his country as a missionary. He was 23 years old. On that occasion, Hiko Futo Hito Gata Du Mon Mikoto, the official portraitist of the Imperial family, made a picture of him. That picture was kept for nearly twenty centuries among the treasures of the Koso Kotai Jingu.

I mentioned earlier the Freemason to whom I spoke about Moses. We also talked about Jesus, and he told me that the Freemasons have knowledge of a visit Jesus made to East India. I knew this, as I had seen in Madras the temple he created there.

One day, without telling him what it was, I showed this historian a reproduction of Christ's portrait and asked him if he knew what it was. He took his time, measured, counted, and studied the different symbols shown on and around the man's figure. After about thirty minutes, he told me that this was a picture of Jesus Christ, dressed as he was the first time he came back from the East. I then told him the portrait came from the Takeuti documents and showed Jesus on the day he received his title from Sumela Mikoto. He jumped up from his chair shouting: "We knew about India, but not this!" He was surprised, but there was no doubt in his mind that the picture was authentic.

There is a great deal of interesting material in the books published by Colonel Yano, Mrs. Yamane and the Takeuti family — too much for me to quote it all. I must stop somewhere.

I only want, in this chapter, to present the most important missionaries of our times, those who founded the main religions of the modern world. I also want to show that traces remain of their relationship with Hinomoto Kuni.

They were all educated in the ancient world center; their words and actions were always based on the Kototama Principle. They could not talk directly about it since their mission was to hide it. If their teaching is looked at in the light of the life principle, the link is very clear.

I will say once again that history is a very unsure science, and that there is much in the work of the historians that I cannot agree with. Their research can provide a starting point, but the rest must be found in one's inner sense of the principle.

I am absolutely sure that the Kototama Principle is the source of all the theories taught by our ancestors. Moses and Jesus both spoke from this viewpoint. This is why the Bible says that Jesus is the son of God. God is its name for the final principle of the truth of human life, the creator: the Kototama Principle. The intelligence, the personality of the founders of our religions came from the Kototama Principle. So it is indeed true that they were the sons of God.

I should add that none of the details of the life of Jesus are mentioned in Colonel Yano's book. He speaks only of Christ's birth in the Middle East. Of course, he wrote that passage in prison just before he died in 1932. He no longer had access to the documents and Mr. Takeuti had not yet made the find he communicated to Mrs. Yamane.

The current head of the Takeuti family has published a "World History of the Era of the Gods" which gives exactly the same information about Christ as Mrs. Yamane's book. She published her work in 1964, Takeuti Yoshi no Miya published his in 1970. Mr. Takeuti must have used Mrs. Yamane's book as a reference. Since so many original documents were burned during the war, we have to rely on Mrs. Yamane's extensive research.

I said I would not quote any more material from the historians' books, but I will go back to Mrs. Yamane's book for one more thing.

Apparently, Jesus left Japan several times. His mission in the Middle East was finished. He seems to have worked a great deal in Japan itself, but he also traveled and taught in other lands. The Takeuti documents record that the fifth time he came back, he returned through North America, arriving with three disciples.

Jesus died in the village of Herai at the age of 118. His tomb can still be seen today. In that region, the funeral ceremonies include special customs which are not found anywhere else in Japan. They belong to neither the Buddhist nor Shinto traditions. There is also an old song of the province...in the Hebrew language.

Mahomet

> "Amatu Kuni, Kamitu Kuni, Hinomoto Kuni, Toyo Ashi Jara no Mizu Ho no Kuni — Amatu Kuni Sumela Mikoto.

In the 32nd year of Bin Tatu, 31st Emperor of the Kami Yamato era, Mahomet was born in Alabia Kuni Meka Siria".

In other words, during the reign of the 31st Emperor of our era, Mahomet was born in Mecca, in the Syrian region of the Arabian world.

> "In the second year of the reign of Jome, 35th Emperor of our era, on May 28th, Mahomet, now 24 years old, arrived in Hinomoto Kuni, landing at Tamba Yukihama Harbor."

These events are more recent than the ones we have already reviewed, and the record is very detailed. The first night, Mahomet slept in the house of Ohira Tarosuke in the village of Inada, close to the Kami Akari Omojin shrine, in the region called Amakoshi ne Naka Hitama Kuni. He was then given the use of a guest house, or perhaps a neighboring house close to Ohira's home.

When Mahomet arrived, he already had the title of king. His

route as he came to Hinomoto Kuni is described: he passed the shores of Goa and Tatukahamo, visited Seito, Taijin, Tenshin, Hoten, Shunsen and Seishyu in China; then embarked from Fusan (a Korean port) and landed in Hinomoto Kuni at Tamba Yukihama.

While he lived in Inada village, Mahomet went every day to the Koso Kotai Jingu to pray in the Besso Koto Wake: the outer shrine dedicated to the ancestors of foreign lands.

The year following his arrival, on February 28th, Ohira Tarosuke introduced Mahomet to the head of the Takeuti family. Mahomet became his student and began to study, among other subjects, politics and the ceremonies of the ancient Shinto ritual.

The master must have been pleased with his pupil: the documents record that Mr. Takeuti made a special request to the Emperor, asking to be allowed to teach more to Mahomet — in other words, to train him as a missionary. The Emperor replied with much kindness and gave his permission.

In the eleventh year of the same reign, on April 27th, Mahomet paid his respects for the last time to his teacher and to the Emperor. He thanked them, said farewell, and returned to Mecca.

In the entry of July 16th of the nineteenth year of the reign, Mahomet is reported to be living in Mecca and teaching his religion. That year corresponds to Kuti Hejyu, the 6th year of the Moslem reckoning.

Mahomet died in the fourth year of the reign of Kotoku, 37th Emperor of Kami Yamato Tyo. He left his mission in the hands of Abu Beluk, his chief follower. In his will, he left orders for Abu Beluk to go to Hinomoto Kuni as his representative, with his greetings to the Takeuti family.

Abu Beluk tried to obey. He left Mecca but died on the road almost immediately. On August 8th of the following year, fifth of the reign of Kotoku, an emissary did arrive in Hinomoto Kuni. His name was Bairu, and he had been sent on by Abu Beluk when he found he could go no further. Bairu went to see the Takeuti family, prayed at the Koso Kotai Jingu, was received by a minister of the government, and finally was allowed to pay his respects to the Emperor. This is recorded by Takeuti Okuni Omi. Generations later, the then head of the family, Takeuti Korimitsu, notes in the margin of this chronicle: "This is a very strange story."

This is a summary of Mahomet's story as it is told in Mrs. Yamane's second book, "The True History of the World". The introduction to this book says a very important thing:

> "The Takeuti documents, very secret records of the Heaven country, are divided into three parts: **TEN**, the Book of Heaven, **TI**, the Book of Earth, and **JIN**, the Book of Man. Until now, all that has been published about the Takeuti documents has been taken from the "Heaven" group of documents. It is recorded in the documents themselves that the "Earth" texts, recording the story of the different regions of the world, are hidden under the ground.
>
> As to the Book of Man...in the Greek mythology, for example, the names of the gods come out without order, and their stories are told haphazardly. But once the Takeuti Book of Man is opened, everything will fall into its proper place. The gods and their representatives will take their exact places and everything will become clear."

I will repeat once more that I am not a scholar, and that my work is not the study of ancient documents. I do not accept the historical books as they are, even the ancient chronicles of world history. I have quoted passages from the books of the experts who have studied the Takeuti documents, knowing that the documents themselves have been altered, added to or cut over the millennia. I believe the work of these scholars can give important indications to those who are looking for the truth of humanity's origins. I also believe that the best way to know anything about the times of our ancestors is to follow the indication of John:

> "When all things began, the Word already was. The Word dwelt with God and what God was, the Word was. The Word, then, was with God in the beginning, and through him all things came to be; no single thing was created without him. All that came to be was alive with his life, and that life was the light of men."
>
> (the gospel according to John, chapter 1:1-4).

Take this path, and try to find the contents of the Word. I believe this is the only way to find out the truth about our ancestors. This is my way of studying history: by standing on the viewpoint of the Kototama Principle.

The Three Principles of Kototama

f we follow the Amatu Iwasaka order of sound rhythms, if we search its contents and grasp them completely as the total content of the a priori dimension, we can see the real nature and activity of the human capacity, here and now. Our ancestors understood this completely and created three principles.

They began by dividing the activity of the a posteriori desires into two categories: the physical and the spiritual. That is the activity of the a posteriori human being.

But is this the total capacity of a living human being?

In what way did these capacities appear, in what order were they manifested?

Our ancestors continued to search and to practice for a long time with their utmost concentration — and they finally found the key.

It was a way of practice which made it possible to see the content of the order of the manifestation of human life. This is the chart of Amatu Iwasaka.

They followed this order from the present physical existence in **U** back to the source, and from the source in **I-WI**, through the eight motive rhythms, back to our physical existence. And they structured the following three principles of a posteriori manifestation.

Amatu Kanagi

The a posteriori human being living according to this principle recognizes the physical senses and their desires as "I am". For him, they are the totality of his self; he recognizes himself only as their expression and acts only from the inner desires of **U** dimension. That is the total content of the consciousness of this dimension.

When the Kototama Principle was hidden, Kanagi was symbolized as the principle of the number 8: the sword that cuts into 8 sections. In the Kojiki, it is Susano wo no Mikoto, the star god, the god of violence. This is the basic principle of the creation of the materialistic and scientific civilization. It is the source of that type of expression of the human capacity.

Amatu Sugaso

This principle is also the content of an a posteriori capacity, but this time, it is the activity of our spiritual side. Our ancestors grasped the manifestation of our spiritual activity from the a priori world to the a posteriori human manifestation, and created this order. It is symbolized as the principle of the number 9, or as the moon goddess: Tsuki Yomi no Mikoto.

Amatu Sugaso is the part of human capacity which creates religions, philosophies, arts. It is the origin of this viewpoint, approach and desire.

Together, these two principles of human activity guide our present civilization. Our society's activity is carried out in these orders. In neither of them however can the direct content of the fifty sounds of Kototama be grasped.

The missionaries who hid the true Kototama Principle created symbolic structures which left hints of its real meaning. Today, we have become incapable even of understanding the content of the two a posteriori principles.

The symbolic explanations of our ancestors could not be too easy to decipher. If we had seen through them, we could never have taken the scientific civilization to its perfection. But the people who made these symbolic explanations knew the full principle.

Without the full knowledge of the complete principle of life, from the a priori source of our self to its a posteriori manifestation, it would have been impossible to structure Amatu Kanagi and Amatu Sugaso.

The human being who grasps the complete content of the human capacities, from a priori to a posteriori, is a god-man.

Amatu Futonolito

This principle is the complete order, it is the totality of human capacity manifested from the a priori to the a posteriori as the fifty sound rhythms of Kototama. It was structured with the practice of Amatu Iwasaka.

Amatu Iwasaka shows the inner action of the seventeen hidden gods (the a priori life rhythms) and the way in which they synchronize with each other. These rhythms appear in the a posteriori manifestation as the basic human capacities: the 32 child sounds.

Our ancestors completed the Amatu Futonolito order and called it the principle of the number 10. In the Kojiki, it is symbolized as the sun goddess, Amaterasu O mi Kami.

About ten thousand years ago, our ancestors hid the principle of the sun goddess. All that remained of the Amatu Futonolito principle was the trace of ancient practices of sun worship. Sometimes the sun was a god, sometimes a goddess. This principle could not be spoken of, even symbolically.

The Amatu Kanagi and Amatu Sugaso principles were also hidden. These orders of the fifty sounds were presented as gods, or alluded to in parables which make up practically all of the ancient epic or religious narratives of our civilization.

Many missionaries contributed to the creation of these symbols and their creations were handed down through the years until the present day. What has reached us is only the symbol, not the principle behind it. The founders of our civilization were only allowed to speak of Kototama in references, and even then, they could only leave references to Amatu Kanagi and Amatu Sugaso.

Once again: it is impossible to understand Amatu Kanagi and Amatu Sugaso without having grasped the complete principle of Amatu Futonolito. Neither Kanagi nor Sugaso has the capacity to see the complete 50 sound rhythms as the content of our life. It is impossible to create these orders without a complete grasp of the principle; therefore the god-men who perfected these orders were standing in a higher dimension. They had a complete, direct knowledge of Kototama.

When I say that you cannot understand Kanagi and Sugaso without a complete grasp of the order of Amatu Futonolito, I also mean that you cannot use them to guide the people of a society. The ordinary people of the first civilization were blindly groping in the direction of materialism. The missionaries had to be able to direct and structure their efforts. They had to help them to stand on the materialistic viewpoint as well as on the parallel way of philosophy or religion. They could not have done this without the complete principle.

The Old Testament speaks of Yahweh as "Almighty God". The content of this God is actually the Amatu Sugaso principle. If we write down the mother sounds in the Sugaso order: **A O U E I**, and say them aloud beginning with **I**, we find **I A O U E** = Yahweh. Yahweh was the spiritual justification of the Hebrew nation's materialistic mission.

Saint John says:

> "When all things began, the Word already was. The Word dwelt with God and what God was, the Word was...through him all things came to be".

This is not something that can be written lightly. He is speaking of creating life, developing civilization, by the power of language. It is impossible to say this without knowledge of the Kototama Principle. The "Word" is the sound rhythms by which human beings can express the actual rhythms of life. That is one of the clearest references to the principle left to us by our ancestors.

If we struggle on without the key to the inner dimension of our life, we cannot escape from the confusion of this society. We cannot purify the polluted environment of the earth.

The founders of the modern civilization were all educated in the Kototama Principle. They were all talking about it in their different ways and presenting it as the "Word" of different gods. The reality of these gods can only be found in the life rhythms of our inner capacity, grasped and pronounced as human mouth sounds.

That is the word of god, that is the complete, the true source of human civilization. There is no other way to manifest it.

The Amatu Kanagi Sound Chart

WA	LA	YA	MA	HA	NA	TA	SA	KA	A
WI	LI	YI	MI	HI	NI	TI	SI	KI	I
WU	LU	YU	MU	HU	NU	TU	SU	KU	U
WE	LE	YE	ME	HE	NE	TE	SE	KE	E
WO	LO	YO	MO	HO	NO	TO	SO	KO	O

This order is practiced from top to bottom, starting at the right, and from right to left, starting at the top.

These are the life rhythms which constitute our physical dimension and its desire of expression. This activity exists in every human being. It emerges naturally and expresses itself first as the physical senses and their desires.

Through practice, we must improve the level of our inner consciousness. If we do not see clearly how limited this dimension of knowledge is, we cannot realize the existence of our deeper capacities. In this dimension, we only have access to the physical or material viewpoint. That is not enough. Who am I, what am I? These are real questions, and we must try to open our inner doors and see the deeper dimensions of our self.

In the Amatu Kanagi sound chart, the order of the mother sounds is **A I U E O**. This means that the source of our life intelligence manifests itself in our a posteriori life in this way. From this expression of life, the a posteriori being cannot recognize the existence of the a priori life dimension.

The beginning of the a posteriori consciousness is the awakening of the five physical senses. When the human body is separated from the mother's womb and comes out into the a posteriori world, the consciousness of the physical senses awakens. Each time we wake from sleep, our consciousness opens anew. Each time, at the very instant of the awakening of the physical senses, we come face to face with the world of phenomena.

The phenomena encountered by the physical senses are already separated into different dimensions: colors, sounds, smells, ... Our own a priori capacity of judgment, the **IE** dimension, has made them separate, and has awakened the consciousness of our physical senses in the **WU** dimension. This awakening belongs to the a priori **A** dimension. It is through this activity that the consciousness of the a posteriori **WU** dimension's physical senses can awaken, face the phenomena and recognize them as they are — already separated.

Everything that comes before: the separating action of the **IE** dimension and the awakening of consciousness by **A** dimension — cannot be realized by **WU**. It never occurs to that dimension to wonder how it wakes up and how it sees the surrounding objects.

In the **WU** dimension, you only know that you exist. You can realize the existence of your own physical senses and of your immediate environment. This environment is limited to the formed phenomenal world which can be grasped by the physical senses.

The actual content of these phenomena changes with every passing second. Phenomena are only temporary, like a reflection in water. They dissolve, disappear, die. That is not real existence.

We see phenomena as real and solid, but they are made of life rhythms which cannot remain immobile a single instant. This is also true of human life. At every moment, the rhythm of our inner life changes.

With the capacity of the **WU** dimension, we see the phenomena — that fragile passing picture — as real, permanent existence. The physical senses can never see the changing contents of the life rhythms of phenomena.

In this dimension, our own grasp of ourselves is physical. What we call "I am" is merely that which sees the phenomenal world. We face the finite world and synchronize with it through the capacity of our physical senses. The memory of this experience becomes our knowledge in **WO**. The content of this capacity is **WU WE WO**: the expression of the consciousness of three dimensions, guided by their inner desires. The content of this expression of life, grasped and structured as a principle, is the order of Amatu Kanagi.

As you have seen in the above sound chart, the Kanagi order of the mother sounds is **A I U E O**; the order of the half-mother sounds is **WA WI WU WE WO**. In the Kanagi order, the a priori inner capacity of the five mother dimensions cannot be recognized. We cannot see the activity of the life dimension's consciousness. We cannot even realize the content of the half-mother sounds **WA WI WU WE WO**.

The half-mother sound rhythms are the activity of the five a priori dimensions in the created human constitution. At the time of this manifestation, each part of the body has already been given the capacity to act, to separate and to judge, on its own level. The sense, functions and activities of the body are separated into dimensions of life rhythms. An **O** dimension kidney cell is completely different from an **A** dimension nerve cell.

Our physical senses appear because the a priori life rhythms are manifested through our sense organs. Our perceptions are the manifestations of these rhythms. The a priori mother rhythms of the five dimensions create the body and manifest themselves as the five senses. That is the order of the manifestation of our physical life.

The viewpoint of the physical senses can look no further than the senses themselves. It cannot reach back to the origin of the senses, it can only turn outward toward the objects perceived by them. "I look out at the phenomenal world". That "I" is the only I to be reached in this dimension.

The mother sounds are the total life dimensions of universal space; the half-mother sounds are the life rhythms of our physical body. The Kanagi viewpoint cannot even realize the half-mother sounds. On this level of consciousness, we only know ourselves through the information gathered by our physical senses.

We feel, obscurely, a sense of self. That awakening is the sound rhythm of **WA**. We wake up and feel "I am alive". That is **WA**. "I can see the phenomenal world" — the phenomenal world is also **WA**. "I can see, taste, touch, smell, hear with my physical senses". That is still the expression of **WA**.

This expression of life is all based on the **WU** dimension physical senses. In their distinct, separated form, they belong to the **WE** dimension. They synchronize with phenomena and grasp the existence of this synchronization. What we memorize then is the picture, the external appearance of phenomena. This memory of the senses' experience is each individual's **WO** dimension.

This means that we are guided by the desires of the **WU WE WO** dimensions, and by their consciousness of our self. The consciousness based on this manifestation cannot have a clear judgment. In our daily life, we only feel a vague desire for more, an occasional yearning for a greater knowledge of self.

This capacity is the consciousness of the Amatu Kanagi principle. For the people living in this dimension's world, it is the only consciousness of the total capacity of the fifty sound rhythms. Every human has the total capacity but the people of this dimension cannot wake it up — they do not know that the total capacity exists. The consciousness of this dimension's capacity can recognize neither the **U** mother sound nor the **WU** half-mother sound. It only knows the eight child sound rhythms in the order of: **KU SU TU NU HU MU YU LU**.

In **E** dimension: **KE SE TE NE HE ME YE LE**
In **O** dimension: **KO SO TO NO HO MO YO LO**

This total of 24 child sounds is the content of the consciousness of the human being who believes "I am" is the five physical senses themselves, and the desires of those physical senses.

Humans are superior to animals by the capacity of their **A O E** dimensions. Animals do have emotions, some imagination, and a great deal of intuition — probably more intuition than most humans because their life often depends on it. Humans usually don't develop this capacity. It is only sharpened by extreme situations, in times of war, for example.

Animals have only the judgment which enables them to escape from danger. Human judgment is completely different: it can put each thing in its proper place — and so create a civilization.

If the **AO** dimension is greater in the human capacity, the **E** dimension morality and judgment does not necessarily follow suit. **AO** is by definition more developed in human beings but our **E** dimension is often lower than that of animals. Animals are not criminals. Human beings, in the pursuit of their interests or in the name of their desires, very often are. In present society, human intelligence and knowledge have almost completely lost the judgment of life.

To leave behind the criminal form of intelligence which can make humans worse than animals, to build a perfect, free and peaceful society, the most important thing is the development of the **E** dimension. **E** is the capacity of morality, or judgment. Its rightful place is above the capacity of the **AO** dimension. The high moral sense and true judgment of the **E** dimension is the highest, most important capacity of humanity and of the universe.

Our modern materialistic civilization is guided by the knowledge and viewpoint of the Amatu Kanagi principle. This principle is the basis of most modern people's understanding. The dimensions held the highest then are the **WU WO** capacities: physical strength, material power, and the knowledge based thereon: science.

All our education is based on the memorial capacity. Every school directs its efforts to developing in young people a strong competitive sense, a good memory, physical strength. Students are expected to have the brain of a computer and to be good at sports. Champions play tennis for two hours and are paid hundreds of thousands of dollars. For boxers, it only takes half an hour. To show more clearly where their values are, the big business companies use these champions for their advertising campaigns. Today, every one, in every facet of society, is rushing along the same road.

The development of the **WE** dimension is missing from our education. Common morality is deteriorating and there is more and more criminality in the young people. If they want something, they take it.

Our most basic values are criminal. It has become impossible for most people to judge what is right or wrong. We are guided by the desires of our physical senses and we use a criminal intelligence to gratify them. The result is what we see around us in the world today.

The content of the Amatu Kanagi principle is the most common viewpoint of humanity today. The most common perception of modern people is to recognize themselves as their physical desires. The fulfillment of these desires becomes a human "right," and the very definition of freedom. If someone tries to control your actions, that is a violation of your most basic rights. The first priority is to protect your own life and its desires. Your freedom is to kill to protect yourself. From this viewpoint, it is impossible to realize that every other life is as important as yours. If you are capable of killing, every other life is probably more valuable than yours. The real criterion is the importance or value of a life to society. There is in the Kanagi viewpoint no real judgment, and no respect for life.

If you have killed someone, your lawyer will come to court to give all sorts of reasons why you should be spared. The value of life is not the issue here, the point is to see who will be most clever, the quickest in repartee, and who will make the best personal impression on the jury. If you are put in prison, the government feeds and clothes you. Criminals follow this to its logical conclusion and protest because conditions in jail are not good enough. Politicians then argue about how they can be improved.

How will this improvement be paid for? The public must pay more taxes. That is only normal, since the viewpoint of those inside and outside prison is the same.

It is impossible to build a peaceful society on the materialistic viewpoint. The Kanagi current spends its money and energy only for the development of the **WU** dimension capacities: for the competitive sense on both the physical and mental sides. It has no notion of the development of the highest capacity, the creator's judgment: the **IE** dimension.

This is true of all the cultures of the world today. They cannot realize **E** dimension. They are based on the activity of the physical senses and on the knowledge of those experiences. They can never realize that the source of our self, the source of life, is the five a priori dimensions. That is our true capacity.

The Kanagi order of the a posteriori five physical senses of **WU** dimension is separated from the real self, it is cut off from the source. It tries to live independently and develops its **WO** dimension knowledge exclusively from the materialistic viewpoint. We become a civilization of orphans. How can there be real knowledge on the basis of only one dimension? How can there be real judgment?

The judgment based on the intelligence of our **IE** life will can never commit a crime. It can never go against the law of life. Judgment based on **WO** knowledge of **WU** dimension can do nothing else but create a society like ours.

I feel it is vital to make this clear. This is the essential point of this book, this is the reality of our present civilization.

I have explained that the a priori **U** sound rhythm is the natural intelligence of human capacity, at its first awakening. It is the very first moment, the gray light before sunrise. When **WI** life power turns to expansion, **U** is the ultimate concentration just as it reverses its direction, springing out into the life will of **I**. It is the first outward impulse.

That moment of **U** dimension, natural life intelligence is still chaos. There is no light yet, it is not possible to separate self from phenomena. There is no subject, no object, everything is merged. This is the **U** sound rhythm, source of the creation of the human body.

In that same moment, the consciousness of the physical senses awakens in **WU**. The **U** life rhythm is also the source of these a posteriori physical senses. That is why, when we practice the Amatu Iwasaka order, **U** is the very beginning, the single original

146

"god" of the universe. It is the source of creation; it creates the human body, consciousness, and the manifestation of human life intelligence.

The physical senses in their different ways, only explore the surface of phenomena. Our sense of touch is the **U** dimension of the physical senses. The sense of touch re-groups all the other senses. The other senses are only branches, subdivisions of the basic sense of touch. **U** is always the central core from which the other dimensions branch out.

When we make the sound charts of the three principles, we divide this dimension into the **U** mother sound and the **WU** half-mother sound to make the explanation simpler. The mother is shown as the subject, and the half-mother as the object. There is in fact no separation in this dimension. There is no possible consciousness of subject or object: it is the absolute beginning of the manifestation of physical life and natural intelligence.

The most common mistake of the Kototama practicant is to think that the sound of **U** is the same thing as the physical senses. This is not true. The life rhythms of the a priori dimensions synchronize with the entire phenomenal world, finite and infinite. The mother dimensions **A O U E I** synchronize with all the energy of the universe. The rhythm of that synchronization itself is received by the a posteriori physical constitution — by the cells, the organs, the sense capacities. Our entire being catches that rhythm and synchronizes with it.

The a priori rhythms appear in this a posteriori synchronization, pass through the body, and are sent by the nervous system to the brain. The brain receives that rhythm and translates it into a picture. The large brain (cerebrum) is like a screen for the expression of the a priori life rhythms. The origin of this screen, with its receptive organs and sensors, is the **U** dimension.

The other dimensions spread out from this foundation. **U** is the source, not the physical senses themselves. **U** is also the source of the spiritual manifestation — it is the source of all living manifestation.

Our body is like a television. It is perfectly made but it is useless without the current of life. Switch it on, the current starts circulating and its first manifestation is a hum. There is no picture yet and no differentiated voices or sounds, but the capacity is there. That hum is the sound of **U**. Then you press the button for a channel, and pictures and sounds come out. That is the capacity of the half-mother sounds **WA WU WE WO**.

The human body is much more intricate, subtle and complete than any machine, but it is still a very elaborate television set. This television set believes that it is the subject: "I am the creator. These pictures on my screen are reality, I created them, and that is the only real existence."

The television does not know that it is showing signals beamed from a central station.

I have explained that our large brain is like a screen. Pictures, sounds, desires appear on that screen, but the capacity of the Amatu Kanagi dimension cannot see its own source. "Where do these pictures come from and how do they appear to me?" That is impossible to realize.

The people living in this dimension cannot see the origin of their desires. They can only see their body as a kind of machine, without any other function than simply being alive. They have no consciousness of who is "I am". Their universe has no coherence. They look around them and try to understand, one by one, the phenomena that appear to their physical senses, without ever finding the link between them. They dig, dissect, analyze, spend all their energy in defining each phenomenon without ever finding the common law of all existence. The automatic result of this activity is the creation of the present, material and scientific civilization.

All I can give here is an explanation, and it is probably not very good. To understand the reality of this society, everyone must try to grasp the content of the fifty sound rhythms of Kototama. Grasp this content in your self, then read my explanation of the content of the Amatu Kanagi principle again. Compare it with what you have grasped and I believe you will understand what I mean.

In the consciousness of this dimension, the **U** sound rhythm of physical desires becomes the subject. The main desire of this dimension is concentration, the collection of outside elements. The five physical senses reach outward, but their activity is the bringing back of elements to nourish and gratify the needs of the body.

These physical desires in themselves are not criminal. The normal desire of the physical body is to collect as much as possible. Once we have acquired something, we want to hold on to it. This something must become a permanent property. We hold on to our life as hard as we can; we hate dying. That is a natural feeling, it belongs to the **IE** dimension of life will and judgment. But at the end of concentration, we must return to expansion. That is the law of life. If our activity only goes in a single direction — if we only take and never give back — we are breaking the law. It is the same as wanting to breathe in without ever breathing out: normal life becomes impossible.

The strongest time of concentration belongs to childhood. The body needs to collect a great deal of outside energy to build itself and to grow. As time passes, the gravitational strength weakens. In a normal human life, desires weaken, the impulse to acquire weakens, as does the will to live. That is also natural. Our society, with its dream of eternal youth, is trying to escape from this law. It wants to remain forever in the child's gravitational sense.

I have tried my best to explain this as clearly and as simply as I could. It is difficult to choose the right words, I cannot find them in the knowledge of my **WO** dimension. I am not completely satisfied with my explanation, but I do not believe I can do better.

The question is not whether the explanation is good or bad. The Amatu Kanagi principle exists in the impulses of every human being, in their inner sense. It is what guides the present-day activity of both individuals and society. You must grasp this for yourself, with complete certainty — know it with complete confidence. That is what I mean by grasping it inside yourself. Once you have seen the content of this principle, you will automatically understand what I mean.

The missionaries who founded our civilization gave the Kanagi principle the name of Susano wo no Mikoto, star god, god of violence. Once you have grasped its content completely, you will see why they defined it with those particular symbols. All your questions about our society will be answered.

The Amatu Sugaso Sound Chart

WA	NA	LA	MA	YA	HA	SA	KA	TA	A
WO	NO	LO	MO	YO	HO	SO	KO	TO	O
WU	NU	LU	MU	YU	HU	SU	KU	TU	U
WE	NE	LE	ME	YE	HE	SE	KE	TE	E
WI	NI	LI	MI	YI	HI	SI	KI	TI	I

This order is practiced from top to bottom, starting at the right, and from right to left, starting at the top.

This is the awakening of the viewpoint of the **A** dimension. In this dimension, the activity of spiritual intelligence is seen as "I am". This is a higher level of consciousness than that of the **U** dimension. Our ancestors grasped the activity of the **A** dimension capacity and created the Amatu Sugaso principle.

This order is **A O U E I** for the mother dimensions, and **WA WO WU WE WI** for the half-mother sounds.

It could also be said that **A O U E** are the a priori subjective capacities, and that **I** is the subject itself. This manifestation of subject and subjective capacities, from a priori to a posteriori, can be called the human "spirit". I have been using the word "capacity" very often. By capacity, I mean the essence, potential, spirit and intelligence of a dimension.

The half-mother sounds of the a priori objective capacity: **WA WO WU WE** can be said to be the objective intelligence, and the sound of **WI** the object. It is possible to divide things in this way. But once one begins to speak in these terms, one immediately falls into a philosophical argument on the meaning of the words. The words of our language are symbolic in any case: they have no innate meaning. From the viewpoint of the Kototama Principle, this type of wrangling with words is only a game of **WO** dimension. You may call it spirit or intelligence, it is still a manifestation of **I-WI**'s life activity. In the process of its manifestation, it creates the human body, and this existence allows it to appear as the human spirit or intelligence. I am not writing a philosophical treatise; for me, all these meanings are included in the word "capacity". If I had to define exactly every nuance of my meaning, we would never get back to the Kototama Principle.

Every human being has his own knowledge of philosophy or literature. If you cling to your references and try to read this book through the filter of what you already know, you can never grasp my meaning. Try to let go of your previous knowledge and to sense the inner meaning of what I have written.

The truth is the fifty sounds of the Kototama Principle and the life rhythms of the sounds. Talk about this in philosophical, spiritual or scientific terms and it inevitably becomes a symbolic explanation. Our artificial languages are completely cut off from the dimension of the life will. The meaning of what we say is intellectual, individual. The sounds by which we name phenomena have no relation to their rhythms. We do not speak from the judgment of the **IE** dimension, but only from our memorized knowledge in **WO** dimension. Our languages are cut off from their roots, they are sounds without life.

This way of discussing the Kototama Principle in a book is like dissecting a dead body. You can accumulate a great store of knowledge on how it was put together, but you won't know what made it live. After you have read this book, you will be no nearer an understanding of the dimension of peace. It will not help you live inside your inner garden of Eden. To reach this dimension, intellectual study is no use at all. Worse: that type of **WO** dimension intellectual knowledge comes to be regarded as a valued treasure. You hate the idea of losing it — the prospect of being stripped of it terrifies you. Out of that fear, you make a prison and lock yourself in it. Your own egotism shuts you in.

The four mother sound rhythms **A O U E** are the subjective capacities; the **I** sound rhythm is the a priori subject. Call it a dimension or what you will, you will find no word that is precisely correct. The only name of **I** is **I**. The true content of the Amatu Sugaso principle is the five mother sound rhythms in the order of **A O U E**. That is the a priori capacity of humanity. There is no point dissecting it into its different aspects and functions. The reality of it is only in the sound rhythms themselves.

The fifty sound rhythms of life are expressed in the brain. That activity is called Mani, Mana, or Man. These fundamental rhythms, pronounced as sound, are Kana, the word of god. That is the entire truth.

The viewpoint of the Amatu Sugaso order of mother sounds still cannot grasp the a priori world. It can see farther than the physical world since it can recognize spiritual phenomena. But it cannot reach the source itself.

The viewpoint of the Amatu Kanagi principle can simply be called the **U** dimension viewpoint; Amatu Sugaso is the **A** dimension viewpoint. The origin of both is the life will **I**, as it passes through the human body on its expansion from the void. In our body, it creates the capacities of both the physical and the spiritual senses. The **I-WI** dimension creates the capacities of the living human body.

A dimension desires, **U** dimension desires immediately face the phenomenal world. The **U** dimension sense is to seize, to swallow, to gather in. The **A** dimension desire is to reach out, as far as possible, passing through the phenomena in an endless expansion. The capacities of **U** and **A** dimensions act in opposite directions.

The capacity of **A** dimension is the light of life. Its function is to light up the chaos of the universe. The entire space of the universe is lit by the **A** dimension light. This is made possible by the expanding activity of the life will's eight motive rhythms. They synchronize with everything they meet — with every expression of universal energy. If there were no phenomena in space, there would be no synchronization and light could not occur.

A can only light universal space because there are energies, or phenomena, to light. If there is no object, there can be no subjective capacity. If nothing synchronizes with the eight motive rhythms, there is no phenomenal world, no light, no existence.

The frontier beyond which there is no more phenomenal energy is the farthest reach, the outer limit of the universe. It is the end of expansion, the end of human capacity and therefore the end of the universe. There is no way of knowing how far this limit is, since it is the end of the capacity of life itself.

Up to now, we have always spoken of the "**I-WI**" dimension. But these two different sounds make it seem as if it is possible to divide the source of human life in two. You cannot separate breathing into inhaling and exhaling; if either of these actions is performed alone, it is no longer breathing. Breathing is one act in two complementary directions. Our heartbeat is a contraction and a release. **I** and **WI** are the two phases of a single life activity.

My teacher, Sensei Koji Ogasawara, named the activity of **I-WI** together "**KI**". For me, that is not exactly right. **I-WI** can only be **I-WI**. I think he wished to make only one sound to name the activity of life, and took for this a concept from China: T'Chi. In the Chinese language, that means "life emerges". I do not believe there is any need to make **I-WI** into one sound. **I** is enough; there is no need to pronounce **WI**.

TI is the **I** dimension's first action. **KI** appears, already on the physical side. **TI** is a spark. With **KI**, the original spark meets something and bounces off. There is a change, an interaction, a creation. In **Kana**, there is a meeting, and it is grasped and named.

I is **I**. **I** already means **I** and **WI** together, the concentration is implied in the expansion.

One name for our Kototama life therapy is Inochi. **I NO TI**: the first action of life.

The Amatu Sugaso principle is founded on the **A** dimension subjective capacity. In this dimension, this capacity is awake as "I am". The action of the **A** dimension capacity becomes the light of life. Then, as the sun when it rises and lights up the world, all the chaotic space of the universe is lit and defined. This light goes as far as expansion itself: it is expansion. It reaches the point where there is no more existence, nothing more for the eight motive rhythms to separate into dimensions, time and space. It can go no further.

The **A** dimension is also finite, even if its scope is infinitely greater than the dimension of **U**. **A** reaches the end of space, the limit of life recognition. But it is not in the capacity of the **A** dimension to recognize its own limit. **A** can only light; it is the **IE** dimension which recognizes. The eight motive rhythms synchronize, light and recognize the limit of the furthest expansion. **IE** divides, recognizes and judges the finite worlds of **U** and **A**. That is the activity of the eight motive rhythms (**E**) of the **I** life dimension.

In the order of the Amatu Sugaso sound chart, the mother sounds are **A O U E I**, the half-mother sounds **WA WO WU WE WI**. The **I** dimension will be expressed as: **TI KI SI HI YI MI LI NI - WI**. The Sugaso principle is the capacity of **A** dimension. It guides us into art, into religion. But the capacity of recognizing the source itself is still missing. **A** cannot realize **I** or its eight motive rhythms.

If you look at the Amatu Sugaso fifty sound chart, you will see that this viewpoint recognizes first the subjective capacity of the four mother sounds (in the order of Amatu Kanagi, this is impossible), then the eight child sounds of each dimension. This makes a total of thirty-six sound rhythms which can be recognized as the existence, the content of our self. Standing on this viewpoint, we will see and recognize the phenomenal world as: **A TA KA SA HA YA MA LA NA**. We will separate it in this way and recognize it.

The spiritual and physical "I am" cannot merge into one. They are separate, standing back to back and looking in opposite directions. Theirs are conflicting desires. **U** says: "I want to eat", and **A**: "I can't be bothered with mere physical needs. I don't care if you die, I want to search out there in the spiritual world". And **U**, naturally, answers: "Fool, if I die, you die too".

Both these dimensions are right according to their lights, both exist here and now, but they are always at war. Their desires are incompatible. They must always compete to see who will be the master. In fact, the physical side always wins. Meditation, fasting, ascetic practices have their limits — the desires of **U** do not. Sugaso cannot master Kanagi, but it must try — and go on trying. That competition is one of the pillars of Kanagi.

And Kanagi fights back. The reason the Jewish leaders wanted to kill Jesus was because he was talking about the Sugaso principle.

I have explained the viewpoint of the Sugaso Principle, but as I have said before, it is not possible to reach the final truth of Kototama with intellectual **WO** dimension knowledge. However well you understand the theory, it won't save you. It can even add to your difficulties. Such a long time has passed since the Kototama Principle was hidden — eight to ten thousand years with no possibility of studying it! Modern humanity has completely forgotten the viewpoint of our ancestors. We do not know how to practice anymore.

Some people are beginning to wake up and to feel attracted to this study. No one can understand the significance of the principle at first, but there is a sort of inspiration, a spark: this is right.

At first, the greatest difficulty lies in the fact that it is not an intellectual study. You must grasp it for yourself through practice. You must suffer before you are capable of standing in Naka-Ima and facing the phenomenal world. It is not easy to leave all your intelligence, all your knowledge behind, and to enter the void like a newborn baby or a blank page. You cannot stand in Naka-Ima with your diplomas or your titles. It is the void, and you must be void to enter it.

This is very difficult, and it is only the first step. But the practicant must continue holding on to his patience and his courage. Slowly, this viewpoint will become a habit. It can be approached either physically or spiritually; it may be easier physically, since we can touch the physical phenomena. Stand in Naka-Ima until there is a synchronization between you and the world of phenomena. You will begin to feel the rhythm of this synchronization.

How does this synchronization occur? Why do you feel this stone is cold, warm, rough, or wet? Nobody can help you, you must find for yourself how this synchronization is possible. Your teachers can only tell you what to look for, they cannot make you find it. Once you grasp it for yourself, you will know what they were saying.

The spiritual approach is more difficult, but the method of practice is the same. Stand in Naka-Ima, facing the natural phenomena. Make this a regular habit. I don't like the word "meditation" very much because it is a religious term. Try to place yourself in the void, facing the phenomena, and to grasp how the synchronization is made.

Once you begin to grasp this, you feel so grateful and so happy. You have found your way back to the garden of Eden. You look at humanity as it struggles and suffers blindly and you feel a great compassion. You want to help other human beings to free themselves. Once you have found this, you can never lose it again.

You look back at your own life and you wonder why you needed to suffer so much. This is an important question, and you must try to look at it carefully.

"I was born in the present-day society, in the current of the Amatu Kanagi principle. A little later, with my education, came the awakening of my emotional senses and of Amatu Sugaso religion. I was trained for the development of the capacities of both the spiritual and the physical viewpoints, and I became a prisoner of the **WU WE WO** principle of Amatu Kanagi and of the **A O U E** principle of Amatu Sugaso. I was entirely caught up in the conflict between the two viewpoints. In trying to sort out the claims of each, I suffered for many years.

I have always had from my youth the desire to search. I was always curious and interested in different approaches, but I could never reach beyond the phenomena to find the source. When I was told of Amatu Futonolito, there was a thick gate barring the way. I could not know that I had put it there myself. I could not pass the flaming sword.

This is why I have suffered so much."

Human beings are born from the a priori to the a posteriori world. They begin to act as a posteriori living beings with a posteriori capacities. Their first activity is guided by the desires of the physical senses. These are of course the expression of the life will and life power, working to build and to hold together the physical body. In this time of childhood, the **WI** dimension gravitational, constructive power is strongest. The life will and judgment of **IE** appear to a posteriori beings then as the **U** dimension — mainly as the **WU** subjective capacity and desires.

Once the construction of the physical body is finished — or nearly finished — about the age of puberty; slowly, the **A** dimension spiritual capacity appears. The five spiritual senses and their desires open out more strongly. They come to their full capacity after the body stops growing. At that time, the content of the **A** dimension should, if we followed the natural human development, become stronger than the **U** dimension gravitational desires. The mental and spiritual sides reach their full dimension and the human being becomes a "thinking animal".

That would be the normal evolution of the a posteriori human capacity if we were not slaves to the material, scientific civilization. Most people today spend their lives in the prison of their Kanagi material desires, locked in by their **WO** dimension education. The people living in "primitive" societies have a more natural sense — but they are often slaves of the spiritual side.

In nature, this evolution is visible in the life cycle of the insect. It begins its life as an egg: turned entirely inward, all its energy is given to nurturing its life. It hatches as a worm and begins to go out in search of its food — to reach out, to acquire and to learn. Then it weaves itself into a cocoon and dreams. It no longer feeds, it no longer has any physical activity. Finally, the complete being, the butterfly, emerges.

Many people — many societies — will die before reaching the highest dimension. If the desires of a human being are limited to the physical senses, he will pass his entire life in the egg's dimension, or at most reach the larva's.

This progression, as illustrated by the insect's life, is the correct order of the development of a posteriori human life. Of course, these capacities all coexist at every stage of the journey. It

156

is a mistake to think that at the stage in which the **U** dimension subjective capacity is strongest, there is no **A** at all. From the moment we are born, we have the capacities of all five dimensions. The five physical senses, the five spiritual senses are all given to us at birth. But when most of our activity is directed toward the desires of **U** dimension, we cannot realize or recognize the activity of **A**. A child has emotions but he is guided by his physical senses. It does not occur to him to examine his feelings. If his mother goes away, he is sad. That belongs to **A** dimension, but he can only realize that he wants her back again.

In the same way, when the **A** dimension subjective capacity is recognized as "I am", even when it is stronger than the **U** dimension desires, these desires never entirely disappear until death. The **U** dimension desires sustain life.

The Amatu Kanagi and Amatu Sugaso principles are the two expressions of the desires of a posteriori human beings. We cannot take two roads at the same time; the desires of each individual must concentrate on one or the other. The other side will not be entirely cut off, but every one must to choose one to guide his life. Each of these roads creates a different type of civilization. The choice of the Amatu Kanagi way of activity will automatically create a material, scientific civilization like ours.

Amatu Kanagi is symbolized as the star god, Amatu Sugaso as the moon goddess. Both of these belong to the night. They are the natural results of the two basic viewpoints of a posteriori life. With only these dimensions of activity, our source — the final judgment of the life will — is lost to us. We have "fallen" from the place of the creator of the physical and spiritual sides of life.

Amatu Kanagi and Amatu Sugaso are natural expressions of life, but they are not enough. If we follow them without the consciousness of our own source, we create cultures without roots, without the knowledge of the life will's desires. No material or spiritual society has the entire truth, neither can give its people complete satisfaction and peace. They can be successful in their creations, make great works of science or art, but that will never be enough. Without the judgment of our source in the **IE** dimension, we will wander blindly, stumbling in the dark, committing crime upon crime without even knowing it. That is why, at the very beginning of the second civilization, our ancestors represented it as a society of the night, lit only by the dim glow of the stars.

The Amatu Futonolito Sound Chart

WA	SA	YA	NA	LA	HA	MA	KA	TA	A
WI	SI	YI	NI	LI	HI	MI	KI	TI	I
WE	SE	YE	NE	LE	HE	ME	KE	TE	E
WO	SO	YO	NO	LO	HO	MO	KO	TO	O
WU	SU	YU	NU	LU	HU	MU	KU	TU	U

This order is practiced from top to bottom, starting at the right, and from right to left, starting at the top.

I have explained several times how the Kototama Principle was hidden by the decision of our ancestors. There are three different orders of the Kototama fifty sounds: Amatu Kanagi, Amatu Sugaso, and Amatu Futonolito. As sound rhythms, Amatu Kanagi and Amatu Sugaso were hidden, but they were still referred to symbolically — in religions, philosophies, and in the oriental practice of medicine. Even in their veiled form, they were still guiding civilization. Amatu Futonolito was completely hidden. The only trace of it is in the memory of the ancient customs of sun worship. No written explanation, no direct reference to its content has remained in our civilization.

The principles of Amatu Kanagi and Amatu Sugaso cannot grasp the complete content of the life dimension. Amatu Futonolito is the only way. We must search for the source of our self in this order of the fifty sounds — we can then grasp the complete content of our capacities as human beings.

The ancient god-men had completely grasped this reality. They only used the orders of Amatu Kanagi and Amatu Sugaso for the mission of the second civilization — to guide the nations toward the development of material and spiritual societies. The principal missionaries of this civilization were the twelve tribes of the Hebrew nation.

When Amatu Kanagi and Amatu Sugaso were symbolized, there remained no reference to the sounds themselves. Still, both these principles were present in every human being, in the natural expression of their physical and spiritual senses.

It is more difficult to grasp Amatu Futonolito. Without Kototama practice, it is impossible to rediscover it. Futonolito is the only road to the final realization.

Once it was hidden, humanity could no longer realize the complete content of its inner capacities. We only had the Amatu Kanagi and Amatu Sugaso viewpoints to guide us.

If we know and practice Amatu Futonolito, we can clearly see the contents of the other two principles. The reverse is not true. If Futonolito is hidden, we have nowhere to turn for the truth.

All the missionaries who left us symbolic allusions to the Kototama Principle tried to give us an idea of where to look for the truth. They knew the complete principle. Later generations, standing only on the principles of Amatu Kanagi or Amatu Sugaso, could not conceive of a higher truth. They took the words of our ancestors literally or rejected them as fairy tales. They had no key to the incomprehensible statements of mythologies or religions. From the beginning of this civilization, we have turned our backs on the truth.

The god-men blindfolded humanity with the veil of Amatu Kanagi and presented their symbolic references as the final truth. We have struggled with these "truths" for eight thousand years, always going back to them and never finding the complete answer to our questions. The god-men have succeeded in the task they set themselves. In eight thousand years, they have guided us into the heart of darkness. They knew before they began what a sacrifice it would be. They can see how far we have come and how much has been destroyed — but this is only a temporary road.

If I may use a negative word, I would say that in the last eight thousand years, our civilization has been completely, beautifully cheated by our ancestors. We have blindly rushed in the direction they showed us; we had no idea of their real purpose. On the basis of their words of guidance, we have destroyed everything around us and sacrificed each other. We have done this to ourselves. And now we are terrified of the results, but we do not know how to stop.

Once human beings begin to understand the Kototama Principle and to compare it with hidden records like the Takeuti documents, we can understand the divine love behind our ancestors' decision.

This is real love, it has nothing to do with sentimental affection. We had to pass through the shadows of this civilization to reach our real selves. We had to explore the material world before we could put it in its proper place and create a peaceful and free society. It is very clear that this was the only way.

We cannot reach the goal without climbing through all the stages of human capacity. To realize fully the source and capacities of the physical and spiritual senses, we had to build societies based on them. This second civilization has been the one to explore the contents of both the Amatu Kanagi and Amatu Sugaso principles.

Between eight and ten thousand years ago, our ancestors, knowing all this, decided to guide their descendants in this direction. They wished to develop it as quickly as possible, and to show the contents of the material approach objectively. This had to be a real, physical experience for every human being: if we go this way, this is what happens. If we are fascinated by our desires or by their objects (the world of material or spiritual phenomena), and forget the **I** source, this is what happens. They felt this clearly and made their decision.

That is not yet the exact truth. Eight thousand years ago, our ancestors still stood within the life dimension's desire and judgment. The life will that is in us, today, has never died from the beginning of time. It has never changed. This means that eight thousand years ago, we ourselves decided to take this road. It was not a choice made by our ancestors as individuals. From a relative viewpoint, we can say: "Our ancestors cheated us". Actually, there is no difference in the eyes of the life dimension. We, the current of human life, put the veil over our own eyes and chose this direction. It was our decision.

In the time of the first civilization, many god-men had completely grasped the content of their "self" — the content of the capacity of human beings and of the universe. They tried, on the basis of this principle, to develop civilization and to create a perfect society. They began to send emissaries all over the world to create local centers from which they could educate and guide the nations in this way. But as I explained before, most of the people of the earth were living with only the desires and knowledge of their **WU** and **WA** dimensions. Neither wanted to leave their viewpoint. They did not want to follow a practice which demanded they leave behind all they had acquired. They loved their achievements in the **UO** or **AO** dimensions and believed they were in the right. If any attempt had been made to force them to open their eyes, they would have said: "No! Leave me alone, I am free to follow the road I choose".

160

There was not only this inability to understand, this passive resistance. The people of the **UO** dimensions in particular threatened the local branches of the emissaries. Wherever an organized society was structured according to the life principle, **UO** people would attempt to take it over. They would try to take their land, to kill the god-men and their followers. The **UO** people felt this to be their freedom and their right. They never stopped to consider why the Kototama societies were more prosperous than their own. They saw good things and came to take them.

At the end of the first civilization, the younger generation of those who had opened the eye of the human seed started asking their elders to reconsider the way in which the principle was taught:

"It is not enough to talk about the life principle and to try to guide people according to its law. They cannot see the principle with their physical eyes. We must show it objectively. We must develop a type of civilization which will show, all over the world, where humanity is led if it lives for the gratification of the individual and of his physical senses.

It is the way of destruction, sacrifice, suicide. We must prove that, and also show that the Kototama Principle is the truth of life.

Let the nations develop the civilizations of the desires of the **UO** and **AO** dimensions. Don't stand in their way or better yet, help them. The sacrifice will be less great if we make it as quickly as possible. Let them have their experience and find out for themselves that the natural desires are not enough."

The elders agreed and the decision was made.

When the activity of life is based on the a posteriori desires of the physical senses, what emerges is competition. Since this competition becomes the most important thing in life, the result is murder, war, suffering and fear. This way of living develops its own education, its own knowledge. It is a vicious circle.

Nobody actually wants this life, though some find excitement in it. You kill to win, or you destroy in other ways, but the victory is never enough. It is just a respite; you know you will be attacked again. One day, you pass the peak of your strength, and you are beaten in your turn. Victory is never permanent, you can fail at any moment. It is the law of life to rise and fall, and everyone grows old.

Everyone inside themselves wishes for peace and freedom, but the present civilization is carrying us in the opposite way. Many people still do not see that this society contradicts every reality of life. Those who do, don't know where else to go or how to make their way to shore.

In the tremendous confusion and suffering at the end of the second civilization, when society begins to understand that it has missed the reality of life, we must start explaining the Kototama Principle again. Many people will understand and put their energies into this search. The complete society can then be built.

Once the people of the earth have had enough of bitterness and confusion, we can begin to present the Kototama Principle again. This time, they will listen and follow it. That was the object of the decision of the god-men ten thousand years ago. On those terms, it was possible for them to accept the sacrifice.

Once again, I am speaking as if we and our ancestors were separate. Their realized judgment was the same **IE** dimension which is at the bottom of us. If you open your own **IE** dimension through your practice, you will see that everything is done by yourself, here and now. The decision, the consequences — we created them both and we blinded our own eyes.

We have suffered for eight thousand years for the development of this civilization. We have committed countless crimes against life. We have stupidly pursued the desires of our lowest dimensions, we have stubbornly held on to their viewpoint. We have punished ourselves enough, it is time to wake up and return to the viewpoint of our ancestors.

Some readers may feel that this has nothing to do with an explanation of the Amatu Futonolito principle. But the key is a viewpoint and not an intellectual comprehension. Once you have begun to grasp the content of the sound rhythms in the Amatu Futonolito order, you will see where the current of our civilization is going.

If we begin to understand the inner content of our self as the content of Amatu Futonolito, we can understand the causes of our world's confusion and suffering. We can also see, very clearly, what is going to happen.

Practice the order of Amatu Iwasaka. Explore it, follow it to the source of your self and arrive at the final seed: **I**, the life will. With the eye of **I**, I can see the very beginning of the manifestation of my self — its birth. The dimension of this birth is the **U** sound rhythm. The world of the **U** dimension is the final, ultimate concentration, the center of the gravitational force. All the energies of the universe come into it. The power which draws them in is the **WI** sound rhythm.

The center is **WI**, the concentrating power is **WI**. From the center point of the **U** dimension, the activity of **WI** turns and goes in the expanding direction. That moment is the birth of our life will, **I**. This is the source of our existence. **I**, acting with eight motive rhythms, expands to the end of the universe. On its way, it synchronizes with all the existences in universal space. At the moment of synchronization, light sparks out, the phenomenon is grasped. This grasping, creating activity is permanent.

I, the life will of human beings, is the total universal life energy itself — but its action goes in the opposite way from ours. It comes into the center of the human body and becomes the spring of human life. This gravitation then returns to the life will of **I**.

When the universal **WI** power changes into one individual seed of life will, this **I** becomes the seer. It begins to create the human body as a sort of receiver, a radar to see its own universal activity. **I**, the life will of individual human beings, is also the life will of the universe. The universe itself chooses to create a mirror to see its own activity, or rather a computer to interpret it and show it on its screen. This is why, in the oriental tradition, philosophers say that the human being is a small universe. The capacity of human and universe is the same. The a posteriori human capacity recognizes the content of its own activity as that of the universe. As individuals, we then create mirrors, radars, televisions, computers — all these are secondary manifestations of the same capacity. In the first stage, the universe creates us as its interpreters. In the second, we scientifically create images of ourselves. Following the viewpoint of this society, our creations naturally stress physical strength and memorial capacity.

That is why Lao Tsu could say: "One creates two, two create three and three create all things". That is another symbolic reference to the law of life. Lao Tsu was one of the best missionaries of the ancient time, and this symbol shows the highest degree of capacity. One: the universe, creates two: human beings. Human beings create the Word, and the Word creates everything. Without the Kototama Principle, how would it be possible to link Lao Tsu and Saint John, who said "All things were created by the Word"? In their different cultures and times, they are talking about the same thing.

The creation of the human body requires the ability to synchronize with the entire universe. We need to collect, to draw in elements from the entire universe. I do not mean material elements but life rhythms. We collect all the necessary elements from the universe and with their help, build the human body. If it did not have all the energies, all the life rhythms in its own space, the human body would be incapable of synchronizing with the universe.

Science has found the universe to have four different dimensions of energy, with a fifth dimension which is the other four all merged together in a central concentration point. Our body is constructed from elements belonging to all the dimensions, all the energies of the universe. Our consciousness is also a life rhythm: the wave frequencies of the large brain. These waves respond to every fluctuation of energy around us. The very rhythm of this response expressed as sound, is the real human language. It is the Word.

The rhythm of the brain is **Mana**. When the waves emitted by a transmitting station touch an individual radio, the sound comes out. When we speak the exact rhythm we receive, as it is, we grasp the a priori world. In that moment, we manifest, we create the universe. That is our capacity: to bring the a priori universe to life in the a posteriori world.

In other words, the energies of the universe create the human body and remain in its core. Their activity continues, identical to itself, in this individual material space. They spiral in and out, spark, synchronize — or are pushed out if they do not belong. In our body, the universal energies have become individual physical life: **I-WI**, life will and life power.

This human manifestation is of exactly the same nature as that of the center of the universe. The activity is the same; the location of the individual center and its power are different. The nature of the gravitational center, whether in the universe or in the human body, is the absolute void. The life energies circle around this center like the winds around the eye of a storm. The universe is a network of interrelated centers, each with its own activity branching out with eight father rhythms and four mother dimensions.

There is no scientific proof of this because science cannot see the activity of the void. A void center is holding together the structure of every one of the cells in our body. The void nature of this center is always the same, but the constitution and energy of the cell is different according to its dimension: nerve cell, bone cell, muscle cell, skin cell, ... The center of each cell is related to the main center, just below the navel, from which our body is created as an embryo. There are other important gravity points like the spiritual "third eye", but the former is the core of all our capacities.

I-WI, the source of human life, synchronizes at every instant with outside energies. In this synchronization, it creates the capacities of the four mother sound rhythms **U A O E**. These are our original human subjective capacities. The activity at the center of the universe is of the same nature as ours — it has the same four mother dimensions. Human capacity is the subject, the seer of the universal activity — therefore its action should be the same. But we grasp it, through our **IE** dimension, as objective existence: **WU WA WO WE**.

Following the Amatu Futonolito order, grasp each of the fifty sound rhythms and make sure that they are your own inner rhythms, one by one. Then you will see the entire content of the life dimension, from the inner a priori content of your self to the a posteriori capacity of life. It is our own inner activity, but we recognize it as objective existence.

Today's education obliges us to study phenomena "objectively". That is the way we have been trained, and "objective" has come to be understood as the only reliable viewpoint. The "subjective" is dismissed because it cannot be proven scientifically.

The scientific, objective viewpoint can only see the surface and never the life rhythms themselves. A doctor can recognize that you are in pain, but he can have no notion of the actual content of your pain. The objective viewpoint cannot understand the constitution of matter: how and why it is as it is. It can only study individual manifested phenomena. It cuts them apart without guessing at the consequences. Each physical manifestation has a living activity, which cannot be disrupted without disrupting life as a whole. Science is incapable of grasping this.

Once we begin to see the living content of each physical existence, it is not possible to destroy it carelessly. Our ancestors, whose viewpoint was that of life itself, placed very different meanings on the concepts of "subjective" and "objective".

The dimension of life, source of our present existence, is the existence of the universe itself. It has no beginning and no end. The source of our life is exactly the same as the source of the universe, and we as individuals live in direct relation to the life of the universe. We are one, there is no difference. The only separation comes from the point of view of the physical senses, which can only grasp the surface and not the inner life rhythms.

The finite phenomenal world exists only through our physical senses. Behind both the senses and the phenomena are the eight motive rhythms. Our eyes, our ears, are only mirrors, beaming back vibrations to be judged by the **IE** dimension. If we misunderstand this, and take the physical senses for the **U** dimension itself, we put them in the place of the subject. Those who believe the physical senses are the totality of themselves cannot reach the real source.

The **A** dimension Amatu Sugaso principle has a different capacity from the Amatu Kanagi **U** dimension principle, but both make the same mistake. The **A** dimension subjective capacities are greater, but they are not the real self. In this dimension, you expand endlessly and lose yourself until there is no way of coming back. It is impossible to realize the complete content of self, here and now, from this viewpoint. Neither can you go beyond the relative existence of phenomena: beyond the difference between here and there, yourself and others.

Once again, both principles are an expression of the life rhythms, but they cannot recognize the word of god. The fifty sounds of Kototama are the basic sounds of all the human languages. There are thousands of dialects on earth and the origin of each is in these fifty sound rhythms — because they are the rhythms of life itself.

In this book, I have tried to outline the content of the Kototama Principle. I have not gone deeply into the meaning of the Amatu Futonolito principle: if you can wake up and grasp it for yourself, you will understand the content of our modern civilization completely, with the eye of the subject. I have tried to give some idea of the manifestation of life, some examples of it as it appears in my understanding.

Once you begin to understand the Amatu Futonolito principle, Amatu Kanagi and Amatu Sugaso will become clear. You will see how different the three principles are. It is only from the standpoint of Amatu Futonolito that you can understand the others. The reverse is impossible.

It is time to bring this book to a close. I will repeat once again because it is very important: the content of the Kototama Principle, studied intellectually — memorized in books or through the words of teachers and put into your **WO** dimension

— cannot help you to survive. The value of this principle is that it brings you to grasp the complete meaning of the fifty life rhythms. You must try to reflect on them, grasp them and wake up your complete self. This principle gives you complete consciousness, complete confidence. It awakens the total human capacity.

I hope every human being will want to practice Kototama and to wake up his inner self. Each human must understand it for himself. While you are only listening to someone else's teaching, you have not really understood: the meaning of the sounds is not yours. You have not really grasped it until you have seen its activity inside of your self.

To finish, I will try to give the final, most important meaning of the Amatu Futonolito principle: the content of the eight father rhythms of the **I-WI** dimension:

I   the life will, the subject.

TI   the first action of **I** as its starts circling, expanding from right to left.

KI   the first synchronization. The expansion of **I** touches the phenomena, creating power.

SI   an arrow cutting straight through the phenomena.

HI   an opening out.

These four rhythms belong to the activity on the side of the subject. The next four belong to the object.

YI   the continuation and expansion of the first spark of **TI**. The permanent space of **I**.

MI   the space of the phenomena touched off by **KI**. The existence of the phenomena.

LI   the spiraling aspect of **SI**. If a direct force meets an object head on, there is an explosion. If both are spiraling, they can roll around each other.

NI   the complete grasp of the content of phenomena. In the Yamato language, Nikiru is to seize, Nimu means "mission accomplished".

The action of the eight motive rhythms is not divided into expansion on one side and concentration on the other. They act as: **TI-YI, KI-MI, SI-LI, HI-NI**.

I should not explain all this, as it will lead readers to believe they have really understood the contents of the father rhythms. I hope it will help guide the research of a few serious practicants.

The life will's first expanding action is the sound rhythm **TI**. It is the first moment of manifestation of natural human intelligence. **TI** sparks out, then expands through **U** dimension, the chaotic phenomenal world of **YI**. It is the continuation of that individual spark which becomes a beam of light through space. This space belongs to the phenomenal world: **TI YI**.

U dimension is the energies concentrating inward. They come in and **TI YI** springs out. The contrary pressures of this meeting create power, which is the rhythm of **KI**. Their moment of meeting is the birth of the light of **A**. **TI YI** is the spark of consciousness, the awakening from sleep. **KI** is the power of consciousness. They create the a priori light, the moment of inspiration. That inspiration is **MI**.

All this belongs to the activity of **I**, the life will, as it expands through the **WI** world of phenomenal energy. The arrow flying straight out is **SI**. Its spiraling action in the expanding direction, from right to left, makes a hole in phenomena. That spiraling action is the rhythm of **LI**.

SI has opened a road through the phenomenal world in 8, 16, 32, 64 directions. It passes everywhere, in every direction, until everything is lit and there is no shadow left in universal space. The universe, entirely revealed, opened and lit, is the sound of **HI**.

NI is the completion: the complete content of the phenomena of the life power of **WI** dimension, is grasped. That which grasps is the life will of **I**.

That is the action of the eight father rhythms of **I**, the life will and **WI**, the life power. That is the content of their synchronization. That is what is symbolized in mythologies as the marriage of male and female gods. They give birth to children — which are the phenomena.

This activity is the highest capacity of human beings. It is the intelligence of universal life, the highest judgment of the **IE** dimension. At the same time, it is the final discerning activity of the creation of the universe. It is the creator, the judgment of the universe itself.

The eight motive rhythms are the essence and the source of our consciousness — the total capacity of human beings. They are manifested by the expanding action of **I**, the life will. They are the highest judgment, creating time, space and dimensions. In this way, they separate and order the phenomenal universe.

The side of the object, **WI**, becomes the energy for the life will of **I**. It exists but it has no capacity of its own, no eyes with which to see itself. It is recognized only by the subject: the **I** dimension. **WI** is the reserve of energy for the activity of the **I** dimension. This is the natural law of the relationship between men and women. You cannot break this law and find happiness. This order must be respected: a woman cannot make the first advance toward a man.

U A O E, the four mother sounds, are a part of the activity of the life will. **I** manifests itself in separate dimensions. The different aspects of its activity are the sound rhythms **U A O** and **E**. That is why I call them subjective capacities: they are parts of the seer, the real subject: **I**.

In their synchronization with the objective side or the half-mother sounds, the four mother dimensions have the same relationship as **I** and **WI**. They are front and back. **WU WA WO WE** are the strength, the power behind the activity of **U A O E**. **WU WA WO WE** cannot recognize themselves, they are grasped by **U A O E**. It is impossible to see one's own back without a mirror.

I have written this book — this very rough explanation — and called it *The Source of the Present Civilization*. If you have eyes to read it, you will have an idea of how this civilization came to be.

We call its evolution "progress" and consider it an improvement over the way our ancestors lived. In fact, our existence is becoming more and more difficult, and we are going more and more against the law of life. Our society is born of the confused knowledge of the dimension in which humanity lives today. The truth and the highest judgment are lost to us.

The purification of this civilization will be the purification of the content of human knowledge: our references, our values, our viewpoint. That is the only way. Society is a mirror of the confusion of every individual. There are no separate problems and no separate solutions. The cure cannot be political or achieved through money or violence. The origin of the difficulties of the present civilization is the content of the human **WO** dimension. Our **WO** is based on the knowledge of the Amatu Kanagi and the Amatu Sugaso principles. These principles are incomplete. Their **UO** and **AO** dimensions are based entirely on the symbolic representations our ancestors made of the principle of life.

REVELATION AT BELLE-ILE

When I was in France in 1989, I went to see the megaliths of Belle-Ile and Carnac. The stones emitted a powerful vibration, both when I touched them and when I looked at them from a distance. It was like the awakening of an ancient memory. I felt the spirits of the ancient Celts were speaking to me. I made notes to keep the experience fresh in my mind.

This inner experience continued when I went back to Paris, and even later when I returned to the United States in October. The feeling of what I had received lasted for more than a month.

I have had spiritual experiences before, but this was like nothing I have ever felt. I am writing it down in the hope that what I learned might be helpful to other people.

What happened interested me even more because of the research I have done in the past in the ancient documents of Japan. Records like the Takeuti documents describe a forgotten, hidden history of the world. I am not very interested in history as such, ancient or modern: we never know how reliable accounts of the past are. But here was a striking similarity. The words the Celtic ancestors spoke to me reminded me very much of what I had read in the Takeuti documents.

At first, I thought I was only remembering what I had read at different times. But some of the things I heard in Carnac are not in the ancient records. I kept on receiving information of the same nature as that which I had found in the ancient records but entirely new to me. It had to do with the history of Brittany when the ancient Celts lived there.

Modern Japanese scholars do not recognize the authenticity of the Takeuti documents. I cannot vouch for the historical accuracy of the detail of either the Takeuti documents or of what I am going to say here. Still, it is very strange that these accounts should be so similar.

True or not, what happened in Brittany interested me greatly and it may interest readers. Readers may interpret it as the fruit of my imagination. I am certain that was not what it was — but I agree my word is not supported by any scientific proof. What follows is a diary of events as they occurred.

8 September 1989

The Kan Nagara Institute in Paris had organized a series of classes on the Kototama Principle and on life therapy at Belle-Ile. There were about forty people in attendance. Toward evening of the first day of class, I suddenly and spontaneously began speaking of the history of the Celts. Belle-Ile had been an important Celtic center, and many of the people in the room were descendants of the Celts. I had not known much about the history of this people — but it was as if their history were put into my mouth.

The students told me there were two megaliths on Belle-Ile which are considered to be the most ancient in all Brittany. There are thousands of standing stones in the region, but these two are like the parents of all the others. The people of the island are very proud of the Belle-Ile stones.

I went to see them the following morning, with the general secretary of the Kan Nagara Institute and our wives.

The two great megaliths are called Jean and Jeanne. Their power was like two tremendous magnets, one positive and one negative, facing each other. Wild berry bushes grew around them. The berries carried a positive or negative charge, according to the sides of the stones on which they grew. It was then that I began hearing the voice of the spirit of the ancient Celts.

At the beginning of the next class, I lit, as I always do, two candles. When I began to pray, I found myself speaking to the Celts. I did not decide this, the words came spontaneously:

"I have come here today to see you; I have brought back the

life principle which you once had".

The candle on my left went down almost to the wick. It contracted to a tiny ball of flame, which neither died out nor flared up again as one would have expected. This was in a closed and crowded room, there was no possibility of a draft. The candle on my right was burning normally.

I waited; the flame continued to hover at the wick, and I began to hear the voices of many ancestors. I felt these spirits were coming to answer me and I thanked them with all my heart. I said:

"I know your nation's history has been hard. You knew this civilization was a civilization of sacrifice — you accepted that. All humanity has suffered, in one way or another. It was all according to your plan, when you decided to create a materialistic, scientific civilization. The goal has been reached. Science has come to the end of the finite world, the end of matter, and is now reaching the infinite.

It is impossible to forget what your nation has suffered in all the years of this civilization. As you can see, the competitive, fighting spirit has run its course. We can return to the final dimension of the life will, and be as you were in your time. We should forgive, forget and build at last a free and peaceful society based on the principle of the human life will. I believe you understand what I am saying. Please help us, with your divine love, to purify this society and to build a better one."

I was praying like this in my heart, and my tears had started to flow. I realized later these were not tears of sadness. What I felt was a great happiness, and a kind of satisfaction. When I finished my prayer, the candle on the right went down in its turn, and actually went out. I felt it was a sign that the ancestors had agreed to do what I asked. It was a miracle; I could not stop the flow of joyful tears. I don't know what the class was feeling, but they were also weeping.

From that moment, I heard these voices more and more. It was as though the ancient Celts were guiding and instructing me. I had planned to go fishing that day, but I completely lost interest in the outing. I had to see the other megaliths, at Carnac.

We arrived late in Quiberon, the harbor on the mainland, and slept in a hotel. The next morning, on September 10, we went to the fields of stones. It was there that I received the following messages, transcribed from my notes:

1) Two great islands (I understood them to be Tami Alai and Miyoi: Atlantis and Mu) sank into the sea 66,800 years ago.

2) These islands emerged again about 36,800 years ago, and 33,000 years later (3,500 years ago), they sank down again.

3) The Kototama Principle was perfected 56,100 years ago by the leaders of the country of Hinomoto. They tried to bring it to the rest of the world to create a perfect society based on the law of life.

At that time, one person among the most advanced of the leaders was elected as the world's guide. This person was called Sumela Mikoto.

Every generation of Sumela Mikoto traveled throughout the world with a retinue of hundreds of scholars and specialists in various disciplines. These became the teachers and guides of the various peoples of the earth.

Among them were the princes and princesses, Sumela Mikoto's children. Sumela Mikoto would give orders for them to remain at the places where they were assigned and continue the work there. They became the rulers and kings of the societies they structured.

These leaders were the Celts. The people who tried to develop a world culture based on Kototama were the ancestors of the Celtic nation.

4) 31,150 years ago, some of the Celts left Hinomoto to settle in the island of Miyoi. The island of Tami Alai was settled 28,500 years ago.

At that time, the Celts sent out as emissaries were traveling over the earth from East to West. The ancestors of the Celtic people of Brittany and England are the descendants of the settlers of Tami Alai. They arrived in Belle-Ile 16,500 years ago.

The natives of the Polynesian islands are the descendants of the Miyoi Celts.

5) The Celts who went West did not travel in search of adventure or for economic reasons. Their purpose was to create a civilization guided by the Kototama Principle.

6) They came by the order of Sumela Mikoto and landed in the areas inhabited by what we call today the Celtic races.

The original emissaries arrived on a ship 12 meters long and 24 meters wide. They were 25, all men. They stopped in different lands on the way and the journey to Brittany lasted four years.

My feeling about this last point is that when they arrived at their final destination, an earlier wave of emissaries had already established an outpost, perhaps on Belle-Ile. The region must have been a wilderness, with a small population of fishermen. The emissaries probably taught them agriculture and medicine. It would be the earliest arrivals who raised the Jean and Jeanne stones.

Jean and Jeanne stand facing each other, North and South, about 250 meters apart. The earth's axis has shifted slightly since the time they were raised: their north is a little to the East of ours.

The thousands of megaliths around Carnac must have been raised by later migrations: none of them can be older than the two on Belle-Ile. The Breton traditions have always made a difference between the ages of these stones.

The Celtic mission was made up of many different groups, some of which came overland and through the Mediterranean countries while others traveled by sea all around the African coast. This migration took thousands of years, during which time they lost touch with each other.

When Miyoi and Tami Alai sank down again 3,500 years ago, the Celts from Tami Alai moved to their European bases, joining the earlier settlers. It seems they came by boat, landing on the Atlantic coasts of France and the British Isles.

When the islands sank, the decision to change the course of civilization had already been made. The Celts who arrived after the disaster, having lost their island homes, must have had great difficulty in following the new, scientific civilization. I feel their arrival must have caused a great deal of confusion.

Before the decision was made ten thousand years ago, all the Celts had been emissaries of the life principle, guiding the peoples of the earth toward a civilization based on Kototama. They taught that this principle was the highest and ultimate truth. Then the material civilization was launched and they began to speak in symbols which only hinted at the truth. In this way, the life principle was hidden.

Now, the most important activity of life was the satisfaction of the physical senses. Human knowledge turned away from the universal law and became the study of how personal satisfaction could best be achieved.

With the hiding of the true principle, humanity fell to the dimension of animals. Its knowledge and skills were those of survival. A competitive society was created in which one had to fight to survive, and it was natural for the strong to devour the weak.

This is still our society today. Using one's intellect to have the edge is exactly the same thing as physical fighting. Human interest has been redirected and human knowledge shaped for this new direction. Human activity has followed. This is the only way to change a civilization.

For thousands of years, the emissaries of Hinomoto Kuni tried to establish a civilization based on the Kototama Principle. The peoples of the different nations could not understand the truth of what they were teaching. A society cannot be perfect if everyone in it is not satisfied. Not everyone was convinced because the ordinary people could not grasp the principle of life without some kind of material proof. The first, spiritual civilization could not provide this. The change to the material civilization was decided upon in order to satisfy this demand for objective proof. Everyone could understand once the activity of life was shown to their physical senses.

I feel that originally, the Celts were not a race or a nation apart. They were simply emissaries, working all over the world. The name of Celts, by which they came to be called, is derived from "seito". In the Yamato language, sei-jin means a pure person, a god-man or a high priest. Sei-to is the plural, meaning a group of god-people. The seito directed a world which did not understand them, and their name came to have a religious significance, as "saint", "santo". It also became the root of the name "Celt".

Once the principle of the sounds is written down in letters, the sounds are dead. Transforming a tradition based on the spoken word into writing was the first major step in reversing the human viewpoint.

Humanity was separated into nations; each group tried to make the best possible society for themselves by destroying whatever stood in their way. The killing of one's enemies has never brought security to anyone. It simply does not work and it has become madness to think it does.

The materialistic outlook cannot make people understand the real, inner sense of the final truth — the pure content of the self as life. The scientific viewpoint is limited to an intellectual understanding. It sees truth from the outside. Everyone can agree about the external appearance of phenomena, but that does not give us their inner sense.

Scientific truth can convince anyone. Most people agree about the theory of the black holes in space, for example, but no one understands their nature. We cannot enter there. The black hole is the source from which springs our life will, the creator of time and space. We can look at it from the outside but we cannot see into its center.

It is our pure self; the source of human life is inside the black hole. As long as we look at it from the outside, we have only a relative view of it. To know it as our own self, we must go into the black hole that is inside of us.

We can explain theoretically the nature and activity of the black hole (and the white hole). We can say that all the universal elements are combined in it and that there is a black hole at the center of every manifested existence: a living cell, an atom, an electron, a particle.

It is possible to understand this theoretically: my body came out of the black hole and will finally go back to it. But this kind of intellectual understanding is not the final truth. It is an explanation of the Kototama Principle but not the Kototama Principle itself. It is only its external appearance. But it is something everyone can understand.

To find the final truth, you must grasp it in yourself. You must go into the black hole and come out again. It is there you will find your true self. Until you have done this, you are only a robot with an intellectual understanding of your own existence. The final truth of your self as the creator of the universe, the creator of time and space, is not an intellectual concept. To see it completely, we must return to the source of life. Then, every human being can grasp the absolute order of the final truth. We can at last create a social structure based on this law.

Before the scientific civilization was perfected, there had to be widespread destruction of nature and humanity. The consequences were faced ten thousand years ago when our ancestors decided to begin the new civilization.

The spiritual civilization had lasted for so many thousands of years, and still not every one could be reached by Kototama. The life principle had to be demonstrated objectively. It is like saying, from the bottom of the heart: "I love you" — and the beloved doesn't understand. And then saying it again, and giving a gift at the same time — then it is understood. We are easily deceived, and we very often confuse love with the gift. But that is the scientific viewpoint.

All existence is grasped from the outside, and that knowledge is stored in our memory. We then say, with great confidence, that we are sure of what we know. We will even fight for it.

This is the way of sacrifice; the truth has been lost. Our ancestors decided to take this road and to spoil our natural understanding — or rather to pass through this civilization and come out with a more complete understanding.

For 46,000 years, the first civilization tried to create a perfect society with the Kototama. It was not possible then. The leaders of the world finally decided to change their approach and to open a new civilization.

The ancestors of the Celts told me this, through the standing stones they raised. They, as the first emissaries of Hinomoto Kuni, were the first to realize the limitations of the spiritual civilization. They were also the first to ask for a change. They proposed a plan, in accordance with the road humanity was taking. A way had to be found to prove the existence of the life principle to the physical senses. People must come to see it, hear it, smell it before they could believe.

It was argued that the peoples of the earth would lose their capacity as human beings. The new society would be a civilization of animals, based on physical strength, winner take all. The leaders of the first civilization could not at first understand how such a sacrifice could be made. But, answered the Celts, after so many years of trying, what else can be done?

All the god-men finally agreed that there was no other way. But who would guide humanity on this road of sacrifice? The Celts had been the first to support the idea, but it was difficult for them to be the representatives of the new civilization. It represented a complete reversal of all they had been teaching before.

They had taught that all human life is one, that no man can destroy another. Now humanity must be told that the strong can conquer the weak, that physical strength and intelligence must be used to gain material power.

It was too much to ask of the Celts. They could not bring themselves to put the new mission into application. Most of them simply stepped back, leaving their places to those who would be able to do what they could not do.

The decision to work on this reversal of civilization was made ten thousand years ago, but it was a long time before any group could be formed to apply it. The Takeuti documents record that

2,000 years passed before the new civilization could begin. This brings us to 8,000 years ago.

The second civilization did not really gather momentum until about 3,300 years ago. The peoples who spearheaded the current may have originated in the area of ancient Greece. I cannot see how the twelve Hebrew tribes were born.

In the Old Testament, it is written that the 12 sons of Jacob were the founders of the tribes, but I cannot take this literally. The Bible is a symbolic record, only hinting at the truth. The peoples constituting the Hebrew tribes came from all the regions of the Middle and Far East. These peoples were the core of the revolution, they led the way into the new era.

They may have been divided into twelve groups. In that case, the name of each of the twelve leaders was recorded as one of the sons of Jacob — or Israel.

These troops were a mixture of many nations and races. It was probably more practical to divide them according to language and customs. These twelve divisions were the army of God.

According to the Takeuti documents, Moses Romulus came to study in Hinomoto Kuni. He agreed to lead the way into the new civilization.

The Hebrews, as the missionaries of the present material and scientific civilization, taught a very different viewpoint from that of the ancient Celts. There is an entire difference between the **WO** dimension knowledge and confidence of the two groups. The Celts had been the vanguard of the first civilization, the Hebrews were that of the second.

Ten thousand years ago, the decision for the change was announced in Hinomoto Kuni and the message relayed to the Celts of Tami Alai and Miyoi. 6,500 years later their islands were destroyed in a geological upheaval. During that period, the new mission caused them great suffering and confusion. They could not embrace the new way. They could not accept the crimes that the new civilization was committing.

The survivors from Miyoi found refuge along the coast of Asia, which had not been flooded. They are the ancestors of the overseas Chinese of today. These are the Chinese emigrants who handle most of the business in the Pacific. Others survived as the peoples of the Polynesian islands. The Tami Alai refugees made their way to the coasts of Western Europe. The Tami Alai Celts were the first gypsies of Europe and Africa. Most of them landed in France or in the British Isles.

At this point, I was no longer sure if what I heard was told to me by the Celts or whether it was emerging from my a priori memory. It had become one voice.

The Celts had been the guides of the world, and they now had to veil what they knew to be the truth, and send their peoples into darkness and degradation. Many lost their spirit and became hopeless and discouraged. A few actually managed to change and join the people of Moses in the new mission.

At the standing stones of Belle-Ile and Carnac, the spirits of the Celts told me that the number of their spiritual and blood descendants is now 35 times greater than those of Hinomoto. They said: "Hinomoto's descendants only make up half the number of the present population of Japan."

There are over 100 million Japanese today. Half of this, or 50 million, multiplied by 35, would equal 1,750 million people. Whether they know it or not, the descendants of the Celts, the oldest nation, are living today all over the world.

The blood descendants of the Celts include: the Greeks, Egyptians, Anglo-Saxons, Vikings, Visigoths, Ostrogoths, Francs, Guroans, Thais, South Vietnamese, Laotians, Filipinos, Indonesians, all of the Middle-East, and the Mongolian and Tibetan peoples.

The peoples of the world can be roughly divided into five lines of descent:

China

India

Arabia

Northern people (Scandinavians, Russians, Germans, ...)

Celts

The Takeuti documents divide the human race into five colors: yellow, white, black, blue, red.

As the influence of the second civilization spread over the world, so did the gravity of the sacrifice. That current has divided humanity into three basic categories:

1. The Hebrew revolutionary nations, who strongly developed the new civilization; today this is principally the business society, devoted to materialism.

2. The people who did not participate directly but who understood the principle. They are the researchers of abstract science, the artists. They create religions, philosophies — all the aspects

of a symbolic, intellectual culture.

3. The people who keep at a distance. They do not belong to either side and observe a strict neutrality. They only try to live as best they can, without contributing to the development of society. These are mostly Celtic peoples.

Whichever type you belong to, you are still part of the material civilization. This civilization runs opposite to the natural law which creates the finite world. It does not create; it separates; it breaks up. Its expression is competition, murder, and sacrifice. Whatever your way of living, whether you participate directly or indirectly, or try not to participate at all, you cannot escape from modern society. The persecutor and the victim are equally offered up in sacrifice.

In our times, all physical existence, be it material or spiritual, is sacrificed in some way.

The leaders of the first civilization knew that in order to reach its objective, humanity must travel a miserable road and be separated in this way. This means that every sacrifice, every destruction of the past 5,000 years has been recognized and accepted by humanity, consciously or unconsciously. There is no tyrant and no victim, no good and no bad. All human beings are equally victims of the sacrifice. There is no enemy; we must all pay. This is the policy of Amatu Hitugi, the human life will.

The Hebrews spearheaded this current. They served it with all their strength and energy. This was their mission; they were the pioneers and they made the greatest sacrifice. If the names of the victims were counted, the number of Hebrews would be by far the greatest.

I explained earlier that the missionaries of the first civilization had two choices: to step back, or to learn to work with those of the second civilization. For the Celts, it was far easier to die than to change their way of life.

There was a hiatus of about two thousand years until the Hebrew tribes were ready to come forward. Then their current got under way and swept throughout the entire world. Every people on the earth now acknowledges material over spiritual values.

This is exactly what the god-men expected. It is the scientific civilization, in which the motor for the improvement of technology is competition and war. The improvement of material science has continued until it has reached, in the last years, the end of matter itself.

Material existence is only a concentration of energy. The physical world does not exist as such. Nothing is actually there, there are only energy waves. For five thousand years, we have believed that material objects have the highest value. The scarcer the object, the more valuable it has been.

We structured a market and assigned a value to gold, to diamonds, all the way down the line to the most "vulgar" elements in nature.

Naturally, we then competed to acquire these things. People threw away their lives to get them. Not only a few people, and not only their own lives: when millions of lives are thrown away for an abstract advantage, that is called war.

Now, science has reached the point where it has realized that matter is nothing. It was something we believed in, an appearance, a mirage. What we call material objects are only a limited space of time and energy; it is only the action of expanding and concentrating forces. When energy becomes more strongly concentrated in a specific space, our eyes recognize it as an existence, an object.

The energy content of all physical existence is exactly the same as the content of the universe. It is nothing to be acquired or sold; it is nothing to fight over. There is no price, no value: because there is nothing there.

For 5,000 years, the **WO** dimension of human mentality has been putting a price on physical existence. We have given everything a price as if it were a reasonable thing to do. Today, science has clearly proven that physical objects are nothing, and such is the stupidity of the human **U-WO** dimension that we continue to compete to win these insubstantial possessions.

Our ancestors foresaw all this when they encouraged humanity to put all of its energy into the satisfaction of material desires and the acquisition of material things. It was not so painful during the transition between the eras but as time went on, the new generations completely lost the ability to search for the a priori dimension. They no longer had any notion of the source of their existence.

The first civilization was over, humanity had turned against the spirit of the leaders of Hinomoto Kuni. If they had been confronted with traditional teaching, the people would have argued: "If materialism is meaningless, then prove it. I am cold, I am hungry, that is real. Of course I want to improve my situation. I want better things to eat."

5,750 years ago, the 12 Hebrew tribes took the responsibility for the material way. I don't believe they always acted together in one area. They must have spread out and pursued the mission in many different ways. I said earlier that the tribes included peoples from all over the East, as far as Asia. The so-called lost tribes returned to their original homes and worked among their own peoples.

One of the lost tribes is Gad, the ancestors of the Korean people. Their mission took them from the Near to the Far East. 3,150 years ago, they arrived in Japan. Most of them settled there and today, half of the modern Japanese people descend from the tribe of Gad.

Gad seems to be the founder of the Yamato nation. Some Celts may also have returned to Hinomoto and worked with the people of Gad. The original inhabitants of Hinomoto Kuni are different from the Celts, their emissaries: they never left Japan.

The people of Hinomoto were said to be the descendants of the gods (Ten Sōn) or the grandchildren of heaven. Heaven is Ana, the a priori world. This means that they had the Kototama Principle.

Gad and his tribe came to Japan as missionaries of the second civilization. They were originally descended from the people of Korea, long ago, in the early days when the emissaries from Hinomoto Kuni had come to build the first spiritual civilization. They now returned with a very different message.

They were of the same race as the people of Hinomoto but their spirit was completely different.

They settled in Honshu and Shikoku, on either side of the inland sea of Seto. They built societies oriented toward commerce, and in a short time, they almost monopolized the economy of Japan. Gad's people are the ancestors of today's Kansei businessmen, the leaders of the strong economic centers of Osaka, Hiroshima, Kyoto. The business practices of Osaka are very different from those of Tokyo.

Japanese society is divided between the control of two groups: the descendants of Hinomoto Kuni in the South, and the descendants of Gad in the North. The people of Gad have made their way to the highest positions. They hold important political and economic posts and have even married into the royal family.

The "Jimmu revolution" marked the beginning of the history of the modern country of Japan. Some scholars of ancient history think the date usually given for this is wrong by 300 years. They place it 2,949 years ago, and I feel these 300 years should be added. It would mean that the Jimmu revolution occurred 200 years after the arrival of Gad.

I received, or rather experienced, all of what I have written here during my visit to Brittany. It was there that I understood that the material-scientific civilization had reached its end because science had come as far as the void. We have come to the end of the physical viewpoint. What can be seen by our physical senses is in fact...nothing.

There is no way to continue in this direction, the journey must end. Science could only continue to search while there were phenomena to be explained. Now that we have reached the end of matter, we will have to turn around and go back. The mission of science was to divide, to break apart. Turning away from that means to work for cooperation, unification.

To define life scientifically, we have separated it. Now we must take all the separate existences and make them one. All existences are one in the Kototama Principle.

It is no longer possible to compete and kill one another; there is no longer anything to gain. The values we set up arbitrarily are no longer to be believed. The only thing of real value is human life. In the end, nothing can be compared to the human life will **I** and its judgment in creating the human body. Nothing in the universe is more powerful than this.

I felt all this when I spoke with the spirits of the ancestors of the Celts. I told them what I had understood and they accepted it completely. They showed their assent when the flame of the candle on my right lowered and went out.

What I have recorded here is what the Celtic ancestors taught me. They told me that all human life is one. All human beings are descended from the same people; it no longer matters whether they are spiritual or physical descendants. In the end, we all return to the spirit — to the void.

The ancient Celts told me that from now on, the current of civilization will make a complete turn about. It will become impossible to control others with material force. We will go in the opposite direction from the one we have followed for the last eight thousand years: we will return toward the principle of human life.

GLOSSARY AND PRONUNCIATION GUIDE

The vowel sounds are open:

A is pronounced as "ah"
I as "ee"
E as "eh"
U as "oo" in cool

Some consonants are slightly different from the English sounds:

SI is almost "shi"
TI is almost "tchi"
TU is almost "tsu"

The sound variously written here as **L** and **R** is a halfway sound which has something of both. Lomyo-Las = Romulus.

Amatu: order of expression of the sound rhythms; their manifestation in the a posteriori world.
Pronounced "Amatsu".

Amatu Futonolito: the complete order of expression of human life.
Pronounced "Amatsu Futonolito".

Amatu Hitugi: the policy of the life will. The current of

universal life mirrored in the expression of our civilization.
Pronounced "Amatsu Hitsugi".

Amatu Kanagi: the order of human expression based on the perception of the physical senses.
Pronounced "Amatsu Kanagi".

Amatu Sugaso: the order of human expression based on the perception of the spiritual senses.
Pronounced "Amatsu Sugaso".

A priori: the world of non-manifested life rhythms. In human expression, that which can be grasped by the spiritual senses.

A posteriori: the world of manifested life rhythms. In human expression, that which can by grasped by the physical senses.

Carnac: famous fields of standing stones in French Brittany.

Celts: emissaries sent out of Hinomoto Kuni in the first civilization to teach the life principle to the peoples of the world. Ancestors of what we call today the "Celtic races".

Child sounds: sounds created by the synchronization between the father rhythms and the mother dimensions.

Dojo: space devoted to practice. Usually martial arts hall.

Father (or motive) rhythms: the eight rhythms of the **IE** dimension, which cannot be pronounced alone: **T K S H Y M L N**.

Futomani:	Full name of the Kototama Principle: Kototama Futomani.
Half-mother sound:	Activity of the five mother dimensions, expressed in the human constitution.
Hinomoto Kuni:	The world center in the first civilization. Name given in the ancient time to the area of the modern country of Japan.
Jikai:	Ten Commandments.
Jingu:	shrine. In this context, ancient Shinto shrine.
Kami Yo moji:	letters of the epoch of the gods. Traditional letters (or Kana moji) of Japan, before the adoption of Chinese characters.
Kana:	Word of God. Exact pronunciation of the rhythm resulting from the synchronization between the rhythm of a phenomenon and the rhythm of the brain. True human language.
Kana Moji:	letters of the epoch of the gods. Traditional letters (or Kami Yo moji) of Japan, before the adoption of Chinese characters.
Kanji:	Chinese characters or ideograms adopted by Japan.
Ki:	force of the **I** dimension. Usually: human energy.
Kiai:	in martial arts, the shout given at the moment of projection of Ki energy.
Ko:	ancient.
Kobunken:	ancient documents.

Ko Shinto:	ancient Shinto, i.e. Kototama. The Shinto religion is more recent, and, like all religions, is part of the veiling of the life principle.
Kojiki:	"Chronicle of Ancient Matters", a mythology completed in 711 A.D. Believed to be the first book written in Japan. Actually a symbolic representation of the life principle.
Koso Kotai Jingu:	the most ancient shrine in Japan, in which were preserved the Takeuti documents. Ancient center of education of the god-men of the first civilization and the missionaries of the second.
Kototama:	the complete principle of the life rhythms. Literally: the spirit of the Word.
Kuni:	ancient term for "country". Refers more to a geographical area, its customs and its people, than to a country as we understand the word today.
Mana, Mani or Man:	the rhythms of the brain; the rhythm of human consciousness.
Moji (or mozi):	ancient term for the written letter.
Mother sounds:	the dimensions of universal energy.
Motive (or father) rhythms:	the eight rhythms of the **IE** dimension, which cannot be pronounced alone: **T K S H Y M L N**.
Nihon Shoki:	other chronicle of Japanese history. Believed to be the second oldest book of Japanese culture, after the "Kojiki".
Ogasawara Koji:	third generation of translators of the "Kojiki" from its symbolic to its original

meaning. Completed and published the work as the "Hundred Deities of Koto-tama". Teacher of O Sensei Nakazono.

Omote: the frontal or direct approach. In this context, the Omote Jikai are the Ten Commandments for the Kanagi civilization.

Sensei: usually: master or teacher. Literally: "He who walks in front".

Sin: true, real. In this context, the Sin Jikai are the Ten Commandments for the Futon-olito civilization. Pronounced "shin".

Sumela Mikoto: the highest of the god-men. The man or woman who perfectly embodies the life will. The guides of the world in the first civilization.

Takeuti: the family of hereditary head priests of the Koso Kotai Jingu. The "Takeuti docu-ments" recording the history of the first civilization were entrusted to their care. Pronounced "Takāutchi".

Ura: the indirect, yielding approach. In this context, the Ura Jikai are the Ten Command-ments of the Sugaso viewpoint.

Other books by this author:

Ancient World History — Translations from the Takeuti
Documents — 1975

My Past Way of Budo — 1979

Inochi — 1979, 1984

The Kototama Principle — 1984, 1992

The Real Sense of Natural Therapy — 1992

To be published:

The Source of the Old and the New Testament

Please direct all correspondence to:

The Editor
2526 Camino San Patricio
Santa Fe, New Mexico USA 87505

Acknowledgements:

Juliette Bouchery — translation

Seie Brigham — editing

Printed by
Piñon Fast Print